A THIRD WORLD

A
THIRD WORLD

DAVID DAICHES

SUSSEX
AT THE UNIVERSITY PRESS
1971

Published by
Sussex University Press

★

Distributed by
Chatto & Windus Ltd
40 William IV Street
London WC2

ISBN 0 85621 000 5

Printed in Great Britain by
T. & A. CONSTABLE LTD.
Hopetoun Street, Edinburgh

FOREWORD

This book is a sequel to my first autobiographical volume, *Two Worlds*, which dealt largely with my childhood. That book, while concentrating on the character of my father, was concerned with the recall of a vanished moment in the history of cultural pluralism in Scotland. The third world of the title of the present volume is the United States: the circumstances of my deciding to go there are told in *Two Worlds*. I hope that, in spite of its lack of the central unifying theme possessed by that earlier volume, the present one will have its own kind of interest. I have tried to avoid putting something down merely because it happened to me, trying to record only what is likely to be of interest (socially, culturally, historically, psychologically) to someone who looks at the whole story from the outside

Chapter i first appeared in *The Southern Review*. Parts of other chapters have appeared in the *New Yorker*.

Burgess Hill,   D. D.
Sussex

CONTENTS

Foreword   *page* v

Chapter

1   Images of America   1

2   Personalities and Politics   21

3   Sympathies   38

4   Farewell to Reverie   52

5   Journeyings   66

6   Interlude for Explanation   87

7   Moments of Unreality   93

8   I Represent my Country   110

9   Life and Letters   127

10 Home   136

11 Culture and Crisis   148

12 Renewal   162

13 Cornell   175

14 Educating the Children   193

15 Entry and Departure   200

    Index   213

Images of America

WHEN I was a schoolboy I wrote and composed a
musical comedy (which was never performed) in
which there was a chorus of American millionaires
and another chorus of American billionaires. That gives a
general idea of how America looked from Scotland in the late
1920s. Later we heard about the Depression and the NRA and
an American fellow-student at Edinburgh University wore a
badge with an eagle on it and said this meant that he supported
President Roosevelt's heroic effort to re-build the American
economy. Meanwhile unemployment was mounting in Britain
and one rainy afternoon, as I was sitting working in the
English Library, I heard men marching to the thin music of
penny whistles and looking out I saw the hunger marchers
—unemployed shipbuilders and miners and others on their
way to London on foot to insist that the Government do something about their plight. America seemed implicated in the
general pattern of economic deterioration, but nobody quite
knew how. She was reproached for not having joined the
League of Nations, but none of us was clear as to whether
this was relevant to the economic issue. Our professor, H. J. C.
Grierson (later Sir Herbert Grierson), went to America to
lecture and came back wearing a new suit which we told each
other was daringly American, though I can confess now that
it didn't seem to me significantly different from the suits he
usually wore. I read *Babbitt*, and Leavis and Thompson's
Culture and Environment, and talked about the damning influence
of the American business ethos and the pernicious effects of

advertising on the use of language. I also read some of the plays of Eugene O'Neill, which intrigued me, and such diverse examples of American scholarship and criticism as Spingarn's book on Renaissance criticism, Irving Babbitt's *Rousseau and Romanticism*, and Robinson's edition of Chaucer, which made me realise that Americans were interested in culture too. It didn't add up to a very coherent picture of the United States.

I knew a fair amount about colonial America—its history, geography, and economy—for history had been one of my special subjects at school and at Edinburgh University an extended essay on Britain's colonial empire in the seventeenth and eighteenth centuries helped me to win the medal in the British History class. But I knew almost nothing of what happened after Cornwallis's surrender at Yorktown, and for a long time there was no incentive to fill this gap in my knowledge. Mussolini's adventure in Abyssinia and the rise of Hitler changed me from a young ivory tower-ist, who would disdainfully proclaim my lack of interest in politics, to an anguished diagnostician of Europe's political and social ills. In 1934 I left Edinburgh for Oxford, where I became friendly with a number of Rhodes scholars who were as worried about the state of things as I was and who saw things in much the same way though of course with a distinct American slant. It was from them, and from one of them in particular, that I got my first distinct image of America.

Perhaps it would be truer to call it not an image but a series of images. How vivid they were, and how well they have survived contact with the reality! There was the Depression, of course, and the whole cycle of boom and bust, with ex-million-aires selling apples on the streets, and there was the fascinating story of the early years of Roosevelt's first term. There were pictures of life on a Midwestern campus, accounts of baseball games, of summer camps, of labour problems, of conflicts between generations (immigrant parents and brilliant American sons, *nouveaux riches* parents and sensitive sons, and many other fascinating varieties). And, from several sources and in great number, pictures of New York City, in summer and in winter, East and West Side, Brooklyn, Manhattan and the Bronx, sidewalks and skyscrapers and drugstores and water-fronts. There were some unusually gifted talkers among these Rhodes scholars, and the New York vignettes with which they entertained me were full of colour and flavour, linked to the daily life of people, linked above all to the idea of the melting pot, of the European adjusting to a new world with all the pathos and heroism that this involved. I formed in my mind's eye a particularly vivid picture of children of Irish or Italian or other immigrants playing on the dusty sidewalks in the hot Manhattan summer, and this picture seemed to me a moving symbol of an aspect of America in which I have ever since been interested. And when one of my Rhodes scholar friends sang "East Side, West Side, all around the town" it seemed to clinch the whole thing: for me at least it projected a vision of children growing up in a world which for them was home—was indeed the world, vivid and real and total—but which for their parents was never quite home, never quite real. I had never heard the song before, and it stirred me in a curious way:

> Boys and girls together,
> Me and Maimie O'Rourke
> Tripping the light fantastic
> On the sidewalks of New York.

It was running in my head when I first looked out on the sidewalks of New York from the twentieth floor of the Beekman Tower Hotel in September 1937 and watched children playing in the bright early autumn sunshine.

I wanted to feel the history. The immigrants I imagined as arriving before the First World War, when immigration was still unrestricted: I saw them coming, from Ireland and Italy and Poland and Sweden, building an American society so different from that of the early colonists which had for so long been my only picture of Americans in action; I saw modern

3

A Third World

America creating itself and saw suddenly and clearly the relevance of it all to the world I knew and the problems I was concerned with. (It was this feeling of mine that later was to give me such a sympathetic interest in Willa Cather's earlier novels.) Several of my Rhodes scholar friends were third-generation Americans, and one was second-generation; and here they were, representing America in Oxford. It was these paradoxes of the Old and New World that gave me my first real interest in the America of my own time.

We sailed to America from Glasgow, my wife and I, on the *Tuscania*, one of those old, slow, Anchor Line ships that took ten days to get to New York. We had been married in Oxford two months before, and this was a joint adventure into a new world. We were both very Old World in family traditions and habits of thought. For my part, I felt the Old World in my blood, in my bones: my Jewish ancestry stretched back to ancient Palestine via Scotland, England, Lithuania, Holland, France, and doubtless other countries as well. I was conscious of the whole history of Europe and the Mediterranean lying behind me. The family name, I had been told, originated centuries ago in Holland. I felt deeply intimate with the European past. To sail to America was in a way to voyage beyond history. Yet when we approached Boston, where the *Tuscania* put in before proceeding to New York, an odd sense of familiarity overcame me. It struck me that New England was after all New *England*, and there were more than the Boston Tea Party and the Puritan tradition to link the new with the old. A curious illusion helped to increase my sense of familiarity. We arrived at Boston on a Sunday morning; first the thrilling view of land on the horizon, then the increasing signs of human activity—a lightship, buoys, smaller boats, and all the while the land ahead becoming clearer and better defined. The buoys were fitted with bells, which rang as they swung in the moving sea, and I was sure that what I was hearing was the sound of church bells from the mainland. There ahead of us lay Boston, on a still Sabbath morning, and across the water

4

came the sound of church bells summoning good New England-
ers to worship. It seemed absolutely fitting. It was only when
the ship passed very close to one of the bell-buoys and I could
see the bell swinging that I realised where the sound was
coming from, but even so I thought that some at least of the bells
I heard were church bells.

To see land after days on the empty ocean is a thrilling
experience, and the greatest moment of a sea voyage of any
length. It is a thrill which air travel (though it has other
advantages) utterly fails to provide. I had the feeling, on
first seeing the American coast, that *there it had been all the time*,
lying all those miles and miles away, with people living and
working; there it had been, completely real, not just a geography
or a history lesson. Through conquering space one had also
conquered time: here was that America which had always
existed. I have since flown the Atlantic in seven hours, but that
is a conquering of space and time in quite another sense. One's
first discovery, after long voyaging, of the physical reality of
another continent is a unique experience. I had a comparable,
yet very different, experience when I flew with the R.A.F.
Transport Command from Montreal to Prestwick in 1944,
having been away from my native country during the earlier
years of the war and dependent entirely on newspapers and
correspondence for a knowledge of how the war had really
affected daily living in Britain. I remember the clouds suddenly
breaking just as the plane crossed the Ayrshire coast, and there
lay the south-west of Scotland below me; *it was still there*, in
spite of the war: it was as though my childhood were still there
after I had grown up. Time and space can be interchangeable
dimensions.

Our arrival at New York on a brilliant September morning
lived up to all expectations. One had seen it in pictures, but
that only increased the sense of having found an imagined
world to be real after all, as though one walked into a house
and found exactly the scene and characters of a familiar
Dutch painting. More exciting to me than the Statue of Liberty

and the great skyline was the increasing sense of involvement in the city as the ship crept up the North River and we saw more of the city's daily activity. It was perhaps unfortunate that we arrived when the American Legion were making whoopee in New York, for this provided an extra touch of extravagance that almost pushed everything back into un- reality again, but the rich life of the city soon absorbed the junketing legionaries and their significance rapidly faded. From one side of our hotel roof we looked down on the East River, busy and bustling and vibrant with life and purpose, and from the other we looked along First Avenue and across 49th Street. We were in a state of high excitement. To see the words DRUGS —SODA—CANDY on a drugstore was marvellous, really marvel- lous: it was so genuinely and uniquely American, and so real and present and right there in front of us. All the varied life of the great city seemed to rise up to me as I looked down, and I was deeply moved.

We lunched at a drugstore for the first time in our lives, and it was there that I first made the mistake that in spite of my subsequent long familiarity with America I still tend to make whenever I re-visit the country. I was asked what I would have to drink—which in a British restaurant means only one thing, an invitation to order beer or wine or something else alcoholic. I didn't realise that I was being asked whether I wanted coffee or milk, and I simply said "no thank you" because we had little money left and were spending it cautiously. The girl's surprised look brought further discussion and dis- covery of what the question meant. We had one of those enormous American sandwiches, and felt as though we were acting out a scene in a Hollywood film.

We could not afford to stay long in New York. We were bound for Chicago, where a teaching position at the University awaited me, together with $500 for our travelling expenses, which in the circumstances I was rather anxious to collect. So the next day we were on our way, travelling by coach and sitting up overnight. (Another difference between British and

American usage: to travel by coach in Britain would mean to go by bus, not second-class by train.) We were told to get out at Englewood Station in Chicago, which was nearer to the University than the down-town terminal. It was a weary journey, and we dozed in our seats, but it had some compensations. I remember looking out of the window in the early dawn and seeing water and reedy meadows with a general impression of a country of lakes and canals. My mind immediately flashed back to a book I had read as a youngster, a book which my mother had received as a school prize in Liverpool when she was a girl. It was a biography of President Garfield, entitled *From Log Cabin to White House,* and it contained drawings of canal and river and lake scenes in the Middle West which I had found oddly attractive. I had forgotten all about the book until that moment, when I suddenly realised that I had read quite a lot about America after all. What about Mark Twain's *Tom Sawyer* and *Huckleberry Finn* and *Life on the Mississippi* which I had so enjoyed as a schoolboy? I remembered now that I had already met America as a land of inland waters, but I had never for one moment associated this America with historical New England or modern New York. This was to prove the beginning of a long process of assembling old and new images of America into a single coherent if complex picture.

We alighted, as advised, at Englewood Station, left our heavier luggage, and set out to walk to the University of Chicago carrying suitcases. We had interpreted "nearer to the University" to mean within reasonable walking distance, and we wanted to save money by not taking a taxi. We found ourselves on 63rd Street on a blazing hot morning. We felt none of the excitement of New York. The street was dirty and noisy, with the elevated railroad blocking the air and light and giving an infernal atmosphere to everything. We felt tired and grubby, and rapidly became uncomfortably hot and sticky. We asked a policeman how to get to the University of Chicago, and we *thought* he replied "Never heard of it". Looking back now, I wonder if he really said that and if we didn't mis-hear him.

We were beginning to discover difficulties with American speech. I asked another man how to get to the University and we had to repeat the question twice before he understood me. To both my wife and myself it seemed that he told us to "turn left at Carriage Row", so on we trudged, looking for Carriage Row. At length we came to a broad street on our left which called itself "Cottage Grove Avenue" and a sudden light dawned. The American close "o" sounds very like an "a" or "ah" to British ears, while American intervocalic "t" is invariably voiced like a "d". What I had heard was "Cahdage" which I instinctively made sense of by interpreting as "Carriage". So I reasoned with my wife, and we agreed that this was probably the street our informant had referred to. So we turned left, and soon found ourselves crossing the Midway with a tower ahead of us that looked surprisingly like that of Merton College, Oxford. It was a relief to get away from the dirt and noise of 63rd Street to a quieter and more spacious quarter.

The University's bursar had sent me a telegram to the ship asking me to meet him on my arrival at Chicago at the Press Building. The first academic-looking building we came to turned out to be the University of Chicago Lying-in Hospital, so we turned away from that and explored further. At last we found a peanut vendor who told us where to find the Press Building. When I inquired there for Mr Mather, the bursar, I was told rather sharply by a brisk woman that if I was a student wanting to register I should go to such-and-such a place. I was twenty-five years old and looked younger, so I suppose her mistake was natural. But I was annoyed. Tired, sweaty, and penniless, I was anxious to find Mr Mather and get settled in, to say nothing of my $500. So I replied rather tartly that I was not a student wanting to register and I wanted to see Mr Mather. She answered even more tartly that Mr Mather was out of town and could not see anybody. At this I produced my telegram and shouted melodramatically that I had come four thousand miles to see Mr Mather and I wasn't

going to be put off. This shook her, and she went away, to
return a moment later to ask me if I was Mr Daiches. I said
I was, and she ushered my wife and myself into the bursar's
office, where we were received in a most friendly manner by
Mr Mather who of course was not out of town at all. He told
us that he had arranged for us to stay at Judson Court, one
of the newer and better equipped university residence halls,
until we could find an apartment, and came with us outside
the building to point out the way there.

Our suite at Judson Court was luxury, pure luxury. (We
thought at the time that the University was putting us up there
free until we found a place of our own, but later learned that
we had to pay $5 a day, which seemed a fearful price to us
then.) We showered and changed and stretched out on the
beds and felt good. Then the telephone rang, and a voice at
the other end said that Mr Woodward, the Vice-President,
would, if I were sufficiently rested after my journey, like to see
me in his office and welcome me; I was told how to get to his
office. So off I went, and found Mr Woodward to be a dignified
elderly man with exquisite courtesy of manner. He welcomed
me with what I would once have called Old World formality
but which I now know to be something very characteristic of
the New World, which in a great number of ways is much more
formal than the Old. (A typical welcoming to a new job at Oxford or Cambridge: "Ah, you're Daiches are you? How d'you
do. Nasty day, isn't it? Have some sherry".) After expressing the
confident hope that I would be happy at Chicago he turned
to more mundane matters and told me that my salary would
be paid in monthly instalments, the first on November 1st, at
which time the $500 promised for my travelling expenses would
be added. I tried not to show my shock at learning I would
have to wait over a month to replenish my now almost non-
existent finances. He must have noticed something, however,
as he added: "That will be all right for you, will it? You have
enough to get along with?" I was so embarrassed and confused
that I thrust my hand into my pocket and pulled out about

eighty cents, remarking, "Oh yes, I have about eighty cents.
I'll be all right." This was not in the least intended as satirical;
it was the result of my youth and embarrassment. Mr Woodward gave me one horrified look, then seizing my arm he
marched me back to the bursar's office and addressed no more
words to me until he had seen the bursar pay out to me $500
in cash. Then he explained to me how I could if I wished bank
all or part of the money right there, at the cashier's office,
which operated a simple banking service for the convenience
of the faculty. After I had, under his guidance, deposited the
proportion of the $500 I did not wish to retain, and received a
small bank book with the amount deposited duly entered, Mr
Woodward put his arm on my shoulder and said gravely:
"Young man, never again say that you will be all right when
you have only eighty cents in your pocket". I returned to
Judson Court feeling enormously rich. I did not at the moment
recall that most of the money I had just received would have
to be repaid to my Oxford bank from which I had borrowed
enough to cover our travel expenses.

With the help of the wife of the Chairman of the English
Department we eventually found a furnished apartment—a
tiny place on Blackstone Avenue, with a bed that let down
from the wall into the living room and a "dinette" and miniature kitchen. This was the first place of our own we had ever
had. It had a refrigerator, and a shower in the tiny bathroom,
and central heating operated by some invisible janitor, and a
maid who came in once a week to clean. It was automatic,
as modern America was expected to be. The image of ourselves living in such a place amused us. In Britain in 1937 only
the wealthiest people had refrigerators; neither of us had ever
used one before. As for central heating, that was as a rule only
for shops and public buildings. On the other hand no middle-
class family in Britain would have been content to squeeze in
to such a small space, to have such a miniature kitchen and
bathroom and only one "public room" as we would call it.
Again, we were acting out something rather than living spon-

taneously. But in a month or two this feeling vanished, and we fell unselfconsciously into an American rhythm of life.

The warm autumn weather, the grey squirrels playing on the campus, the leaves turning, the sense of an academic year starting up, these mingle in my memory as a background to those early weeks in Chicago, where I was simultaneously entering a new kind of university life and a new domestic routine. I was given an office, which I shared with another instructor; I was presented with free copies of the books I was to "teach from" (unfamiliar phrase); I got stacks of free writing paper with the appropriate university heading printed on it. These were all new experiences for one whose only post-graduate academic experience had been an assistantship at Edinburgh University and a research fellowship at Balliol College, Oxford. I was impressed by the enormous anthologies of poems and plays of which I received "desk copies" (another new phrase) and by the variety and novelty of the courses I was asked to teach. (In Britain you give a course of lectures; in America, you teach a course.) I gave a course in drama from the Greeks to the present day, with about a dozen representative plays to discuss and analyse. And there was the real challenge of a course in the modern English novel, which I had never before thought of as something to be taught in a university. Everyone concerned with the teaching of English literature and related subjects was excited about the "new Aristotelianism" which Dean McKeon had propounded and Professor Crane, the Chairman of the English Department, had adopted. The argument about critical principles was fierce and continuous. Within a week of arriving at Chicago I was challenged to reconsider everything I had ever thought about literary criticism.

The students were a lively, argumentative, demanding crowd. I had no knowledge of their background, their general intellectual equipment, or their capacities. I did not even understand the difference between freshmen and graduates (I had a graduate seminar as well as courses for undergraduates) and at first talked to everybody in the same way. Gradually I learned my way about the terminology and the groupings of an American university. I quickly learned to expect no background in classical languages but, among the best students, a passionate eagerness to learn and to think. It was all immensely exhilarating, and sometimes confusing. After I had talked for two weeks on Greek drama, discussing *Oedipus Rex* at length, a girl who had attended regularly came up and asked me whether this was Business Administration 101. I replied that of course it wasn't, it was the course in drama whose number was such-and-such. "Do you mean to say," I added incredulously, "that you have been attending this course for two weeks under the impression that it was a course in Business Administration?" She nodded. "What on earth did you think I was doing?" I asked. "Oh," she replied, "giving us background."

I had only recently celebrated my twenty-fifth birthday, and looked younger than many of my students. Indeed I was younger than a considerable number, especially the graduates. I suppose it was my coming from Oxford that gave me a sort of prestige that my age and appearance would certainly never have given me. I enjoyed discoursing with an air of authority about something I had got up the night before. I worked fast and easily, sitting in our tiny apartment evening after evening working out ideas to present in class the next day. It was a very hand-to-mouth way of preparing lectures, but it has remained my invariable method. I never wrote out lectures, but made brief notes in the margin of a text or scribbled a few reminders on a scrap of paper. In the process I developed a complete theory of the modern novel and much else besides. I doubt if the students realised how much I was feeling my way. But I think they liked me, and I certainly liked them, though they made demands on me far in excess of anything British students would demand of their teachers. I would sometimes get rather tired of having to answer questions about the fundamentals of literature every time I crossed the campus. Students would come up and ask: "What do you think Aristotle really meant by 'imitation'?" "Which do you consider the six greatest novels of the world?" "How would you defend the study of literature?" "What are the humanities and why are they important?" In Oxford it would have been in bad taste to ask such fundamental questions: it was taken for granted that one knew the answers, and one argued with exhibitionist cleverness about details, making all sorts of oblique allusions to works it was assumed everybody had read. In Chicago nothing was assumed, all questions were asked point blank, and you were not allowed to get away with a perfunctory answer. It was exhausting, but valuable.

This was the Hutchins era at the University of Chicago. Hutchins was no longer the "boy president" he had been on his first appointment, but he was still in an evangelical mood and a tremendous force in the University. I had met him at Oxford the preceding June and we had talked about a number of things, and it was as a result of this conversation that I was later invited to teach at the University with the rank of instructor, but with the kind of classes generally given only to senior members of the faculty. I had read his book *Higher Education in America* before crossing the Atlantic, and though I was not then aware of exactly what he was fighting *against* I had great sympathy with what he was fighting *for*. He was against every kind of academic babbittry, and for intellectual discipline for its own sake as mental culture regardless of any vocational or material advantages. It was all perhaps a bit obvious to someone fresh from Oxford, but I could not help admiring his wit and verve and enormous confidence. The trouble with Hutchins, I felt, was that his crusade on behalf of genuine academic culture was conducted in such a sprightly polemical mood that he was led into acceptance of charlatanism if it used the right vocabulary. There was a lot of nonsense talked about "great books" in Chicago at this time (and subsequently), and some of Hutchins's lieutenants were so sold on culture that they became hypnotised by its apparatus and were led into purveying all kinds of obscurantist chat. Feeling for

and against him ran furiously high, and in my first few months
at Chicago I was subjected to the most violent arguments from
those who felt that he was the new Messiah as well as from
those who felt that he was destroying the University. It is true
that he could not always tell an impostor from the genuine
article, that he did not fully understand the place of meticulous
scholarship in university education, and that he sometimes gave
the impression of knowing more clearly what he was trying to
abolish than what he was trying to establish. But, though I was
well aware of these aspects of his character, I could not help
liking and admiring him. He was also very kind to me personally. I remember too being struck by his memory and
powers of observation. When he had talked with me in my
rooms at Balliol College, Oxford, he had been sitting in a
chair with its back to the wall on which hung a picture of my
fiancée, as she then was. When he first met her in Chicago he
said: "Oh yes, I saw your photograph hanging in your husband's
room in Balliol". That he managed to see the photograph to
which he had his back throughout our whole conversation, and
remembered that he had seen it, still astonishes me.

Slowly autumn gave way to winter. Soon after our arrival
we had been invited to an English Department barbecue in
Pulaski Woods, and the high conviviality that took place in
that mellow autumn evening was our first taste of a kind of
academic hospitality we had never met in Britain. Flasks of
Martinis went the rounds with a fine abandon before the actual
meal was served, to the accompaniment of some of the most
highbrow conversation I had ever participated in. I remember
thinking that here at least hard drinking and high thinking
went together. But after the meal was over, and darkness had
fallen, the festivities took a new turn, with singing both by
groups and by individuals. This was the first time in America
that I rendered what was to become my celebrated singing of
"Clementine" in Greek, in the wonderful version by Professor
A. W. Mair of Edinburgh. The whole proceedings seemed to
me a sort of initiation ceremony. I had never heard the word

"barbecue" before receiving the invitation to this affair, and my first reaction was to associate it with the word "bastinado": I thought it was some kind of torture or beating up. It is a measure of the progress of civilisation that the local pub in the Cambridgeshire village where I lived in the 1950s had an annual barbecue, advertised as such throughout the village.

The university faculty did a great deal of entertaining, and my wife and I were thrown into a social whirl of a kind that neither of us had experienced before. Praise of American hospitality to visitors has become so conventional that I hesitate to make the obvious remark that we were entertained with a warmth and a frequency that were quite overwhelming. It was of course all great fun; we were young and ready for anything. We found too that we could make friends—real friends—more rapidly than we had ever been able to do in Britain. Though there is a great deal of meaningless effusive gesturing in American social life, which I came to know much more about later, there is also a capacity for real friendship among "intellectuals" that I had never encountered before, though it may have been a personal accident that this was such a novelty to me.

We had so many debts to pay off during our first year that we had to live carefully. I remember one evening a professor rang up to say that he would like to come round with a friend whom he wanted us to meet. Of course we said we would be happy to see them both. Then I discovered that there was not a drop to drink in the apartment. I went round to the local drugstore, which had a liquor licence (still an astonishing fact to us), to buy a bottle of Scotch, only to find that I had only $1.50 on me. It was the end of the month; my salary was due the following day; meanwhile I was broke. I asked the man behind the counter if he could give me credit until the following day, and he replied that as far as he himself was concerned there would be no trouble at all, but it was against the law to give credit for alcoholic liquor. So I had to buy a bottle of California sherry, a beverage for which I had no great passion, and duly served it up to our guests, who drank it like lambs. On one other occasion that I remember we served California sherry to a guest who dropped in on an evening. The guest and I, talking volubly the while, consumed the best part of a bottle, and no sooner had he left than I became violently sick. I learned later that he had become violently sick immediately on leaving our apartment.

This is not a dig at American wines, in which I soon became interested through Frank Schoonmaker, who opened a wine retailing establishment in Chicago soon after we arrived. He invited a considerable number of the university faculty to his opening wine-tasting, which was staggered over a number of days. I don't quite know why my wife and I were honoured with an invitation on the first day; but we were, and we went with a few friends, and drank our way steadily round a great horse-shoe table of wines. We got merrier and merrier as we progressed, and came to the end in a rather reckless mood. I remember signing some rather odd names in the visitors' book. I had been entertained so often with stories of the appalling sorts of drink Americans consumed during Prohibition—stories told so often with *pride*—that I could not conceive that any American had a palate for wines left, but there were certainly some palates surviving among the academic profession, that profession which everywhere has a more educated taste than it can afford to live up to. I watched with great interest Frank Schoonmaker's early attempts to educate Americans both in the general subject of wine and in the potentialities of native American wines, and when he and Tom Marvel sent me a copy of their book on American wines I began to develop a real interest in American viticulture which I extended over a period of years not only by following the grape-growing experiments of Philip Wagner (and studying his *Wine-Grower's Guide*) and those of U. P. Hedrick, but also by visits to vineyards and wide and exploratory consumption of the products. (I became in fact for a short period wine expert on a Washington periodical, having taken on the job under the impression that I would get cases of wine to review, but all I ever received were books about wine.) I was much impressed by the Sonoma Pinot Noir that Schoonmaker was selling in 1938, the first American wine that made me realise how perfectly the burgundy grape grows in the Sonoma valley, as his Napa Cabernet made me aware of the successful cultivation of the Cabernet Sauvignon grape (which is the claret grape) in the Napa valley. I was of course dismayed by the large quantities of inferior red wines, made from a careless variety of unsuitable grapes, that were shipped in tank cars from southern California to be bottled in Chicago as "claret" or "burgundy", and believed firmly with Schoonmaker that the proper labelling of American wines, using the name of the grape and of the district instead of French or German regional names, was the only way to teach the American public to discriminate among their own wines. I developed a palate for the white wines of the Finger Lakes, which have a quality all their own, and I regretted that the attractive and informative name "Sparkling Catawba" had given way to the ridiculous "New York State Champagne" (but that was not as bad as "Hudson River Rhine Wine"). I could not, however, stomach any of the "foxy" red wines grown east of the Rockies. The Concord grape is an abomination as a wine grape, and even the Isabella makes an impossible red wine, even when bottled under Schoonmaker's label, though, like the Delaware, the Dutchess, and the Iona, it gives a very tolerable white wine.

The American native grapes found east of the Rockies are resistant to the dread phylloxera, which rapidly destroys the European *vitis vinifera* when transplanted there. I became much interested in the various eastern hybrids (the American grapes mentioned above, except the Concord, are hybrids), and experiments in grafting European vines on to American stocks to improve the flavour while retaining the resistance to phylloxera. The French have developed many such hybrids, and American viticulturists have developed their own as well. In California the *vitis vinifera* is not attacked by phylloxera, for reasons which I don't understand, and many varieties grow splendidly; besides the Pinot Noir and the Cabernet Sauvignon there is the Gamay, which I think makes a better wine in the valleys just north of San Francisco than it does in most French Beaujolais, which is made of the same grape. Potentially, America may well be the greatest wine-producing country in the world: if only more American wine-growers would have the patience to experiment over long periods with different sites and soils and not succumb to the urge to mass-produce. The picture of America as a wine-producing country was very different from that of the orgiastic consumers of bath-tub gin which so many of my American friends painted for me with positive nostalgia. I could never understand this sentimental view of the delights of Prohibition, surely one of the most appalling experiments in the history of any society. One result of Prohibition seems to be the large number of Americans who drink just "for the lift" while hating the taste of what they drink. Once, returning to America from a wartime tour of duty in Britain, where Scotch was then unobtainable, I was horrified to find, in the bar at Pennsylvania Station, a group of American soldiers knocking back excellent Scotch mixed with anything they could lay their hands on to take the taste away. I sometimes wonder if the Hollywood convention of indicating that a character is drinking an alcoholic liquor by making him give a horrible little grimace after his gulp derives from the Prohibition view that liquor always tastes horrible and is drunk only for social reasons or for the kick it provides.

In our early months at Chicago, before I had learned about American wines and while our financial resources were still uncomfortably limited, we had to return hospitality with such liquor as we could manage to provide, which was generally beer or cheap California sherry. There could have been no worse introduction to American wine than that sherry, and indeed, though heroic endeavours have been made to produce sound American sherry by the Spanish *flor* process, I have never tasted an American sherry that has real quality. But the baked and caramelised product of the culls of raisin- or table-grapes crudely fortified with raw brandy, which is what we offered our guests, in all innocence, was something much more disturbing than an indifferent sherry; it was an almost lethal weapon.

But it was all living—real, vibrant, engrossing living, growing into a new environment, learning new customs and conventions, cocking an ear for new terms and idioms, settling into a routine which was not really a routine because it was so different from anything we had ever been accustomed to. How well we got to know the feel of those streets between Blackstone and Ellis Avenues running north and south and between 57th and 53rd Streets running east and west, the subdued mixture of residential and shopping and university buildings on 57th Street, the clattering, shamelessly commercial, 55th Street with its noisy street-cars, the quieter 53rd Street, north of which the avenues for a time became more decorous, more determinedly "residential". The apartment buildings—many of which have now been pulled down—had a determined middle-class air about them, with varying degrees of pretentiousness or (more often) of fading elegance. The smell of warm varnish caused by the steam heat, a smell we had never experienced before, is still for me the characteristic Chicago smell. When we installed central heating in our Cambridgeshire cottage in 1956 and it was first turned on when the autumn days grew chilly, I smelled that smell again and was at once taken back nearly twenty years to our Blackstone Avenue apartment in Chicago in the late autumn of 1937, and momentarily recaptured the feeling of novelty and adventure and even incredulity that we of all people were living our daily lives in an ordinary American environment.

We would go shopping in the Loop on the Illinois Central train, waiting on the high exposed platform, oddly primitive in structure and appearance, I always felt, for such a great modern city. There was then no teaching on Mondays at the University of Chicago, and every Monday afternoon we would go on the I.C. to Randolph Street, and wander around Marshall Field's, which I still think is the most exciting department store in the world, or gape about the dark and frantic rectangle of streets and buildings where the true pulse of the city seemed to beat. Then back in the gathering gloom to the by now familiar suburban station, from which we walked home along 57th Street to the almost too welcoming warmth of our miniature apartment. As winter came on, and darkness fell earlier, the contrast between exterior and interior grew ever sharper, and as we walked back from the station past the endless apartment buildings we thought of all the families, each boxed up in its cosily heated and lighted square, and felt so benevolent towards them.

We used occasionally to go to the movies (as we soon learned to call them) at a place in 53rd Street, and I remember one evening just before Christmas of 1937 walking north up Blackstone and being struck by the lighted Christmas trees in the apartment windows. Lighted Christmas trees in windows were phenomena unknown in Scotland, and we were fascinated to see the coloured bulbs in window after window, symbolising not so much Christmas as a determined cosiness, the resolution to be warm and happy. It was not quite our world, and we watched it without envy as outsiders. Occasionally there was a tree with all blue lights, and these seemed especially intimate and domestic, a strangely moving emblem of Chicago apartment life. How far away this was from my chorus of billionaires: here was an aspect of America I had never imagined or anticipated, something which for all its obviousness touched my imagination. I liked those blue trees, and they will always be associated in my mind with our first winter in America. I think now, looking back, that they are in some sense the most American things I ever beheld. It is difficult to say why; one has no control over one's associations. We stood and looked up at them on that cold December night and knew at last that we were in the heart of the United States.

CHAPTER TWO

Personalities and Politics

I HAVE mentioned the smell of warm varnish produced by steam heating in American apartments, especially when it was first turned on in the autumn. We were very warm during our first American winter, in our tiny apartment on Blackstone Avenue where the bed folded up into the wall to allow what had been a bedroom at night to become a living-room by day. It was warm, too, in the somewhat battered wooden frame building—used by the University of Chicago to provide overflow accommodation—where the secretary of the English Department had her office and I had mine, which I shared with another instructor. (I had always associated the term "instructor" with the teaching of physical education until I learned in America that there it was the recognised term for one of the lower rungs on the academic ladder.) I remember so well the smell of warm wood that rose to meet me when I entered the building. Inglewood Hall, was it called? I am sure that it has long since been pulled down. Indeed, within a year it had ceased to be used by the English Department, and I was given a much grander office in Wieboldt Hall, one of the main university buildings.

The English Department was riven by the Great Aristotelian Debate. Soon after we had settled into our apartment Ronald Crane, the Department head, called and presented me with a paper he had written entitled "The Two Modes of Criticism". This, so far as I know, was never published, so I have only my memory to go on in giving an account of what it said. But I am sure that I remember it accurately, as it formed the begin-

ning of a curious on-going debate that I had with Crane over
the years. The two modes were Aristotelian or "meroscopic"
and Platonic or "holoscopic". The former, concerning itself
with the "meros" or part rather than the "holos" or whole,
examined the given literary work as a unique and individual
artefact, discovered its principle of order, and described it in
terms that revealed that principle. The holoscopic method, on
the other hand, took the whole universe into its area of discourse and discussed a literary work in a free-ranging manner
which could include the realms of ethics, politics and biography. He felt that the Platonic or holoscopic method (which
he also called "Coleridgean") had had its day and that its
widespread application obscured the true nature and individu-
ality of works of literature, which were structures of meaning
each with its own pattern of organisation which could be discovered by the use of the appropriate "organon". His essay
was thus a plea for the re-introduction of the Aristotelian
method, which eschewed ethics, history and biography to concentrate on the form of the specific work.

Crane read the essay to me aloud, sitting on the plum-
coloured couch in our living-room-cum-bedroom. I was flattered
that he should have come to me with his essay, but I found his
whole approach unfamiliar and excessively theoretical. Looking
back on the scene now, I find it oddly amusing. There was I,
a youngster from Oxford just turned twenty-five, and there,
sitting opposite me and reading me his essay for my approval,
was Ronald Crane, exactly twice my age, Chairman of the
Department. Crane had a really incisive mind and he always
conducted his arguments with a fine logical precision which
demanded, or so he believed, a terminology more exact than
that available in the language of either the scholar-critic or of
the belle-lettrist with which I was most familiar. I thought his
terms too technical and his language at times jargon. But I
was impressed by his strenuous argumentation, his carefully
worked out distinctions and his unfeigned joy in making a
case. The trouble was, that I myself had just finished an essay

(which later became the first chapter of my book, *The Novel and the Modern World*) that implicitly denied his basic distinction between Aristotelian and Platonic in that it tried to establish a relationship between the principles of formal organisation as well as the other characteristics of a work on the one hand and social and intellectual history on the other. And I had wanted to show *him my* essay. Yet there he was, sounding off to me about critical methodology in a way that made my own critical work seem to represent a total confusion of methods. Or at best I was a mere Platonist, which meant old-fashioned and unresponsive to the needs of the time.

When Crane had finished reading his essay, I said that there were a lot of things in it that I should like to think about, and he gave it to me to read over at my leisure. I then gave him *my* essay, which nobody else had yet seen, which he took home to read. I do not remember our pursuing the argument further at that time. But on many occasions within the next few months we engaged in strenuous argument. In this early evangelical phase of Crane's Aristotelianism he was busy working out conspicuous examples of his method in action. I remember once he explained to me that he had discovered the true principle of organisation in Jane Austen's *Pride and Prejudice*. It was "the progressive exhaustion of co-possibilities". At the outset of the novel a number of possibilities concerning the future behaviour and disposition of the characters emerged, which were one by one exhausted by the development of events until at last only one (Elizabeth's marrying Darcy) remained: and when all possibilities except one had been removed, the remaining one became an inevitability. I said that this was most ingenious but doubted whether it bore much relation to the reasons why experienced and sensitive readers had for generations admired *Pride and Prejudice*. I was always making the point to Crane that literature is valuable because it illuminates life, not simply because it is an ingenious pattern, and he would always reply that the first thing is to see the individual work of literature for what it is. On this occasion I went on to say that the value

23

of *Pride and Prejudice* had something to do with Jane Austen's sense of the dailiness of daily living, her moving awareness of the way in which the reality of human life as it is commonly experienced is built up out of trivia. (I would regard this now as a very partial and oversimplified explanation.) I added that this was how Jane Austen always affected me: and Crane replied that I must distinguish autobiography from criticism.

The Great Aristotelian Debate was often conducted with great bitterness, but never where Crane and I were concerned. It is a curious thing—it strikes me now looking back, but I saw it also at the time—that I was in an extraordinarily privileged position. Crane enjoyed talking with me and often told me his new ideas before he had confided them to anyone else. And I, half his age, would talk with him without constraint. He was always kind to me and spoke with admiration of things that I wrote even though I did not employ his method at all. I was a sort of licensed Platonist. But elsewhere in the English Department there was considerable bitterness about the new Aristotelianism, and about Richard McKeon, then Dean of Humanities, who was regarded as its "onlie begetter". McKeon in turn was held to be a protégé of President Hutchins, so the split in the English Department was related to the larger split between the pro- and anti-Hutchins factions.

Crane was one of the most intellectually stimulating people I have ever talked with, and I remember on many occasions pursuing arguments with him just for the sake of the intellectual exercise involved. In talk (as distinct from writing) I quite often adopted his method and we would vie with each other in finding an appropriate "organon" for the discussion of a specific work. I remember once it was Stevenson's *Treasure Island*, of which Crane had developed a remarkable structural analysis. He was fond of Stevenson, and asked me to give a seminar on his work which led to my book on Stevenson a few years later. It was Crane, too, who suggested that instead of giving a routine seventeenth-century course I should give one on "Bacon, Brown and Hobbes", taking the students in the closest detail through *The Advancement of Learning, Religio Medici* and *Leviathan*. This meant much hard work for me, but I found it immensely valuable. It was in analysing works like these that I found the stimulation of Crane's keen and incisive mind most helpful.

To some, Crane was at this time a monster of opinionated arrogance, but this was a very unfair view. He had many attractively childlike qualities. His shy smile as he awaited a compliment after having developed an ingenious argument, his simple vanity, his happy chuckle at his own jokes, many of us found endearing. He was a great whisky-and-soda drinker, and I can see him now at a party, having backed someone into a corner in order to expound a new idea, flourishing his high-ball as he bludgeoned the trapped guest with subtle logic. He was a kind man, as was his wife Julia: my wife and I received nothing but kindness from both of them. Yet I felt that this was partly because Crane was so pro-British. I had come from Edinburgh and Oxford, and was therefore allowed an independence of view that his own graduate students and young instructors were certainly not allowed.

Crane was a great controversialist, but he was nonplussed if someone to whom he had expounded one of his theories just flatly denied that it was either interesting or relevant. This very occasionally happened, and then Crane would silently take a gulp of his whisky and seek out somebody else to talk to. (I am thinking mostly of occasions at parties: academic Chicago when I was there was extremely sociable.) The most devastating thing that ever happened to him was in our apartment in Chicago, I think some time about 1940, when William Empson was visiting Chicago on his way back from China. Empson had dinner with us, and we invited Crane and some others in for drinks after dinner. By the time Crane arrived Empson, who had drunk a certain amount before he came to us and had continued steadily after his arrival, was beginning to show the influence. Oblivious of this, Crane went up to him and delivered himself of one of his most ingeniously worked out theories, one that he had just perfected and was anxious to try out on a captive audience. I remember his face as he finished expounding it to Empson and waited with a shy yet eager smile for the expected compliment. There was complete silence for about a minute, and then Empson said, coldly if a trifle thickly: "It is people like you who are responsible for the sufferings of millions of people in China". Crane's jaw dropped with shock and anger, and he was speechless. Shortly afterwards Clarence Faust, then a member of the English Department at Chicago though later a big man in the Ford Foundation, offered in his characteristically gentle way to drive Empson to his hotel, to which Empson, with deliberate desire to *épater les professeurs*, said that he was putting up at a brothel in the Loop. He left with Faust, presumably for the brothel.

More than a quarter of a century after our argument about *Pride and Prejudice*, long after I had returned to Britain, I visited Cornell University in the course of a brief lecture tour in America and found Crane there, after his retirement from Chicago, as a visiting professor. He was as talkative and intellectually vigorous as ever, and he knocked back the whiskies-and-sodas even more quickly. But he had mellowed. In the previous twenty years he had both broadened and subtilised his critical method so as to embrace a much larger area than that to which he had at first confined himself, and he was now, in his middle seventies, one of the finest and largest-minded academic critics in America. He had been re-reading Jane Austen, and at a dinner party he propounded his view of her. He talked about the moving quality of her treatment of detail. "Ronald," I said, "twenty-five years ago, when you were analysing *Pride and Prejudice* as the progressive exhaustion of co-possibilities, I said something very like what you are saying now, and you said that to take such a view was to confuse autobiography with criticism." "David," he replied, "if I said that I was wrong." That was a handsome thing to say, something that the Crane of the 1950s could say easily and gracefully but that one would never have expected of the Crane of the late 1930s.

26

Personalities and Politics

At an earlier stage of his career Crane's way of paying a compliment was often to read Aristotelian procedures into something you had written without any thought of Aristotle. In the late 1940s, when I was professor at Cornell, I gave a talk on "The Limits of Sociological Criticism" at the Modern Language Association. Crane was in the audience, and came up to me afterwards to say what a good talk he thought it was. "That was a splendid use of Aristotle's *De Partibus Animalium*", he said. "I don't know when I've heard a better application of the *De Partibus*." I had never read that work of Aristotle, and had no idea of its relevance to literary criticism; but I just smiled and accepted the compliment. I am still bothered by the fact that I have never read the *De Partibus Animalium*.

Crane died not long after his eightieth birthday. In his last years he had made a new reputation for himself as a genial and stimulating visiting professor at a variety of institutions. His mind was expanding until the very end. He began as a bibliographer and textual critic, then moved on to the history of ideas, and made a name for himself in both fields. He was fifty before he came seriously to literary criticism, and it took him some time before he could assimilate the various intellectual schemes that he began by adopting. He is now known as the leader of the "Chicago School" of criticism. But though of course the younger men who were influenced by him in Chicago —Norman Maclean, Elder Olson, W. R. Keast and others— showed that influence in what they wrote, none really possessed his flair or developed his kind of flexibility.

Crane was both scholar and critic, but there were some scholars in the English Department at Chicago who felt that Crane's critical method threatened true scholarship and who in fact regarded him as having wrecked the department. The charge was more often levelled against the Dean, McKeon, who was regarded as originally responsible for this whole development, and bitter words were spoken at university cocktail parties. These words were never addressed to opponents, always to friends, just as those who attacked Hutchins complained about him to sympathetic colleagues rather than to the President himself. This was natural, but it made for a certain air of conspiracy in some quarters. And there were some members of faculty who played both ends against the middle, whispering with the rebels and at the same time courting the administration.

We had friends on both sides of the great divide, not because I changed my views according to the company I was in, but partly because my own critical position was flexible enough to involve ideas and practice from both camps, and partly because we were young and eager for experience and British, three attributes which seemed to appeal to a large variety of members of the University of Chicago faculty. Many of our friends were considerably older than ourselves, from Mrs Edith Foster Flint, who had recently retired as first woman professor of English at the university and though in her late sixties had a vitality and an intellectual curiosity that put many younger people to shame, to Ged and Esther Bentley, who were older members of our own generation and who probably taught us more about America—not formally, but in the course of many casual conversations and joint expeditions—than anyone else. Bentley was primarily a scholar of Elizabethan and Jacobean drama and was not very happy with the Crane régime: he later left Chicago for Princeton, where he still is.

One of the most remarkable friends we made in Chicago at this time was not academic at all. She was Sarah Schaffner, wealthy widow of the Schaffner of Hart, Schaffner and Marx the large clothing firm, and we first got to know her through the Cranes, who were members of the salon that she built up around herself. At the Cranes' dinner party where we first met her there was another guest whom I also met then for the first time and with whom I was to remain on terms of high formal friendship until his death some fifteen years later. This was Giuseppe Borgese, literary critic, scholar, novelist and historian, refugee from Mussolini's Italy, a heavy jowled man of powerful personality and that over-precise pronunciation of English so often to be found in educated Italians. He had just published *Goliath, or the March of Fascism,* the first book he had written in English, a fact of which he was immensely proud. He talked about the book quite a lot at dinner, and was eloquent in defending its thesis that the evil of fascism was an Italian invention and had a long history in Italy: Hitlerism was a bastard version of the original Italian phenomenon. As Borgese was a bitter anti-fascist, I found it surprising and even in some degree amusing to see with what fierce if inverted national pride he insisted on his own country's having produced the original version of this great international evil. But he was not a man with whom one could be facetious. I remember that on this occasion he was talking with denunciatory eloquence of some of Mussolini's crimes when Julia Crane intervened with a light laugh to say, "I guess that so long as you can keep your sense of humour it's all right". Borgese for a brief moment looked darkly at her in silence and then said, in accents of bitter sarcasm, made all the heavier by his Italian habit of inserting a slight vowel at the end of every final consonant: "I am glad that you find it funny, Mrs Crane!" Poor Julia, who had simply wanted to restore good humour and a light touch to the dinner-table conversation, was annihilated.

Borgese could be formidable on social occasions, but I liked and admired him, and we found that we shared a number of prejudices. For example, I always argued that Italian was one of the great classical languages of Europe and that for students of English literature a knowledge of Italian was almost as important as that of Latin and more important than that of French. I inferred from this that Italian ought to be taught as a dead language—by which I meant that students of other European literatures should learn to read fluently the great Italian classics from Dante on rather than study how to ask for a cup of coffee or an ice-cream in Italian. Borgese, who liked a good paradox, took up my point and declaimed eloquently that Italian would live outside Italy only when it was taught as a dead language. As for America, he believed that with the overrunning of so much of Europe by fascism (this was in 1938) the prospects of the survival of European culture in Europe were dim and that it was the European émigrés in the United States that would preserve the true Europe. He quoted Goethe's words: "Hier oder nirgends ist Amerik" ("here or nowhere is America"—the "here" being inside his own breast) in order to reverse them: "Hier oder nirgends ist Europa"—America was potentially the new Europe. He was a deeply European character, who had been involved in political as well as literary and academic affairs in Europe in the years immediately after the First World War. He is the only man who has ever sent me a telegram in Latin. This was many years after I had left Chicago. I had written an introduction to a selection of his English poems which appeared in the magazine *Poetry* (Chicago), and when he first saw it he was so pleased that he telegraphed me: "Poeta criticum amabiliter amplectitur".

But I have been deflected from Mrs Schaffner by Borgese's powerful personality. She used to give lunch parties on Sundays at 1, in her beautiful and richly appointed house at 4819 Greenwood Avenue, and after my wife and I had first met her at the Cranes she began inviting us to these. The Cranes were always there, and Frances and Jack Viner (the historian of economic and political thought who later went to Princeton), and there were a number of other regulars who included people high up in the worlds of banking and politics and any odd celebrity who happened to be around. The ritual was always the same. First, the maid served old-fashioneds, of which Ronald Crane and I, but no one else, were always allowed two. Then we sat down to lunch, which was always a lavish and beautifully cooked meal, with the main course often accompanied in the appropriate season by artichokes, to which Mrs Schaffner was very partial, and nearly always accompanied too by a superb vintage burgundy served *iced*. She had a really splendid cellar, perhaps laid down by her husband, but she knew nothing about wine and left the choice (and the icing) to the maid. It used to break my heart to find the bouquet and flavour of so many noble wines destroyed by having them served straight out of the refrigerator. But I never had the heart (or the courage) to tell Mrs Schaffner that old burgundy should not be served ice cold, and nobody else seemed to care. (I know perfectly well, by the way, that a young Beaujolais can be very pleasant if drunk chilled: but the same does not apply to a 1929 Romanée Conti drunk in 1939.)

The conversation at these dinners was often on international politics, but it always had more the air of international gossip than of serious discussion. Mrs Schaffner took little or no part in the dinner-table talk, but looked around her table with pride as the anecdotes and revelations flowed. Looking back now, I find I can remember almost nothing of this talk. But I remember the general atmosphere, the air of knowing chat which dominated everything. Crane used to love to pick up odd bits of information and proceed, with his fine logical mind, to construct brilliant and bizarre theories out of them. My wife and I were the babies at these parties: I must have been at least twenty years younger than any other of the men present. This didn't, I confess, inhibit me at all, and though I lacked expert knowledge of the international political scene I cheerfully joined in with views and observations.

There was something European about the atmosphere of Mrs Schaffner's house and parties: she came, as her husband had, from a German Jewish family, and she gave forth an air of cultivated liberal scepticism. Her personality was positive, but her views were not. She loved to hear the ding-dong of conversation and argument around her, and on the few occasions when really sharp differences of opinion arose she used to look with a smile from the face of one disputant to that of the other, as though appreciating the scene aesthetically. She enjoyed her wealth, and used it conspicuously and unselfconsciously. If the weather was bad she would send Freeman, her chauffeur, for us with the Cadillac (we never had a car when we were in America). She would have an enormous party on Christmas Day and give all the guests expensive presents.

She was immensely kind to my wife and myself, and we developed a real affection for her—"Aunt Sarah", as we were taught to call her. Yet I somehow felt that we, like her other friends and guests, existed for her as a part of a play acted out for her pleasure and gratification. This did not trouble me, and as I smoked my large H. Upmann cigar after one of her splendid dinners I was perfectly happy to have such crumbs from the rich woman's table. I should mention that she was over seventy at this time, and very active and vigorous: she lived to be over ninety.

Political discussion on the campus was very different from the carefully stage-managed conversations at 4819 Greenwood. I am speaking of our first eighteen months in Chicago, from September 1937 to March 1939, the period during which we first really got to know the United States. This was the heyday of Roosevelt's second term, and it was taken for granted among the university faculty—at least among our friends there, though very different views were maintained among, for example, some of the medical professors—that Roosevelt represented Light and his enemies Darkness. Indeed, there was an atmosphere of left-wing euphoria on the campus that was not unlike the atmosphere I had left behind me at Oxford. It was only a few months after my arrival in America that my book *Literature and Society* appeared, written for Gollancz's Left Book Club at the request of John Strachey. This at once gave me a left-wing reputation among the students, and I was invited to innumerable political meetings where the best means of fighting fascism and such questions as the proper function of the arts in society were furiously debated.

This was the great age of "social significance". I had been involved in this at Oxford, too, when groups of us would meet in Balliol to explore, with quasi-Marxist fervour, all possible social angles of all conceivable phenomena. But in Chicago the atmosphere was different, and the basic reason for the difference was the existence of the New Deal. In Britain student protests against a government which upheld a traditional social system and did nothing either to improve the shabby lot of the workers or to stop the march of fascism across Europe; their demonstrations against the Franco rebellion in Spain and calls for a united front with all elements on the left—all this was shouting in the air in that it bore no relation to what the government was doing or looked likely to do. But in the United States there was Roosevelt and there was the New Deal. There were the "alphabet agencies", like the WPA (Works Progress Administration) in which students were much interested, and political arguments so far as the home front was concerned centred on desirable modifications and expansions of existing developments. Theatre workshops were set up as part of a writer's project within the WPA and we went to see plays like *Waiting for Lefty* to join an audience which watched with a unanimous sense of commitment. When *The Grapes of Wrath* appeared in 1939, with its presentation of the plight of the migrant worker from the Midwest, the interest it aroused was much more political than literary.

The spectrum of the left ran all the way from moderate New Dealers to extreme Trotskyites who saw no difference between Roosevelt's government and Hitler's. A floating pro-communism was in the air, as it had been at Oxford, but since Roosevelt's rabid business opponents regarded him as a communist the term was not used as seriously as it had been in England. Indeed, the whole vocabulary of politics was to the right of the British vocabulary: I had learned in Oxford to use the word "radical" as meaning a mild, old-fashioned kind of reformer who had no place in the modern world, but it was a pretty fierce term in America. There would seem to be a contradiction here—"communism" employed to mean anything left of Herbert Hoover and at the same time "radical" meaning a dangerous red; but there was in fact a simple logic to this linguistic confusion, and that was that the political right deliberately equated every kind of left-wing thought with the most extreme. Colonel McCormick's *Chicago Tribune*, with its extreme right wing, anti-New Deal and anti-British views, preached a kind of pre-Goldwater *laissez-faire* capitalism coupled with isolationism and thus provided daily evidence of the enemy in our midst. We knew of its enormous popularity, and we knew that McCormick spoke, though in his own obsessed and perverted way, for an aspect of the American Dream that ran very deep in the Midwest.

There is a paradox here that is worth looking at. The British, especially after the outbreak of war in 1939, almost unanimously looked at American isolationism as a wicked profascist stance, and hardly any one could have conceived isolationism as anything but politically reactionary. But in fact one strain of isolationism was in the noblest tradition of American political thinking. The United States had been founded in an attempt to free that country from the dynastic wars and iniquitous social hierarchies of a corrupt Europe. After all, it was George Washington himself who had declared in his farewell address that "it is our true policy to steer clear of permanent alliance with any portion of the foreign world". Isolationism in American politics was traditionally a progressive (or left-wing, as we put it today) attitude. Robert La Follette, the great Wisconsin reform leader and Presidential candidate of the Progressive Party in 1924, had bitterly fought America's entry into the First World War, as his son later fought his country's entry into the Second World War. The fight to save the American Dream from the corruptions and sophistications of European power politics is an important part of American history. In the latter part of the war, when I was working at the British Embassy in Washington, I tried hard to make my colleagues see that American isolationism was not identical with original sin, as most of them assumed, but could be the other side of a noble idealism. But of course idealisms themselves become corrupted, or at least involved in forces their original exponents never foresaw. The dream of freedom, self-reliance, simplicity and splendid innocence merged eventually with that of free enterprise and the associated cult of "the bitch goddess Success", the code of the tycoons and the habits of the Gilded

Age; but that cannot alter the fact that the instinctive beliefs to which Goldwaterism appealed only a few years ago were, however confused and politically illiterate those who held them, related at a deep level to a strain of idealism and innocence in American political thought.

Learning the grammar of American politics was a fascinating process. And I learned it from all sorts of people, from Robert Morss Lovett, novelist, retired professor, and veteran liberal, then in his late sixties, to the youngest student who would come to my office and talk to me about his family background and his rebellion against his parents' political ideas. And students did talk. Many of them were little younger than I was, so that they did not feel any generation gap in approaching me. But there was a national gap, which seemed to stimulate their curiosity. I found most of them crassly ignorant of Britain and Europe, but well disposed and intensely curious. The Midwestern student in the late 1930s was much more isolated—even from the east of his own country, to say nothing of Europe—than he is today, when mass student travel has become so popular on both sides of the Atlantic. The more intelligent of them worked hard and read intently, but they found it hard to relate what they learned from books to the living reality. A lack of capacity to *visualise* life outside their familiar environment was continually brought home to me. I remember once, after I had bought a red pocket diary and stuck it in my waistcoat pocket, one of my students came up to me and, pointing to the protruding red top of the diary, said, "Is that an old school tie?" I thought she was trying to be funny, but soon discovered that she wasn't. She had vaguely imagined that the old school tie that she had read about was some sort of coloured decoration stuck on to some part of the wearer's person.

But I liked my Chicago students and made friends with many of them. Some are now distinguished professors, a fact which can cause me embarrassment as well as pride. In 1957 I was lecturing at Indiana University and there met Thomas Sebeok, the linguist, who as a mature graduate student, refugee

35

from Europe, had attended some of my classes at Chicago. He is older than I am, and as he has grown older has acquired an air of venerable wisdom which I have never been able to achieve. Professor Sebeok seized my arm at the party when I appeared and proceeded to introduce me to a number of people with the formula, "I'd like you to meet my old teacher". People turned expecting to meet a wizened old man: I was in fact forty-four at the time. When they saw me, they concluded that this was some esoteric joke of Sebeok's and it proved difficult to explain that he was in a sense telling the truth.

Politics on the Chicago campus were not as sophisticated as they doubtless were at Columbia, but they were *related* in a way that perhaps the political ideas of New York students were not. Chicago, hog-butcher to the world, had the great steel factories of Gary, Indiana, to the south, the dairy farming state of Wisconsin to the north, and the great grain-producing prairie states to the west. Almost every aspect of industry and agriculture was reflected in the city and its periphery. Chicago had, too, its own flourishing if somewhat strident culture, its enormous vulgarities and traditions of violence side by side with its theatres, museums, its Newberry Library and Art Institute. It had its Gold Coast, its tycoons, its Press boss, its epically corrupt local government machine which supported Roosevelt and the New Deal on the national front while remaining shameless and reactionary locally. It had, too, though not in such large numbers as New York, its refugees from Mussolini and, more especially, from Hitler, and in nearby Milwaukee there was an old-established German community. Chicago had its Irish community, its Polish community, its Negro community; the decaying grandeur of the near north side and the frank slums of the west side; the beautiful Lakeshore Drive, commercially prosperous Michigan Avenue, the university community on the south side. It was a true microcosm of America, and every problem, national and international, that Roosevelt was facing in his second term, was illustrated in some facet of life in Chicago and its environs. To

36

look at local politics in Chicago, from precinct captain and ward healer to Mayor Kelly and his machine, was itself an education in American history and sociology. It was not a city I would have chosen to spend my life in. But as a place to live in for a few years, when one is young and curious and possesses an appetite for experience, I don't think the Chicago of the late 1930s could have been bettered. I found it fascinating.

CHAPTER THREE

Sympathies

⊰⊙⊱

ONE of the things that surprised me about the University of Chicago was that it was a great intellectual centre. I had known before I came that the University was a good one, but nobody in Britain in 1937 was able to think of Chicago as a city from which emanated the highest kind of intellectual excellence. It was not only the quality of the thinking that surprised me; it was the passion with which the thinking was accompanied. At Edinburgh University in the early 1930s there had been no great critical or philosophical debates, no spectacular differences in principle among the university teachers which produced opposing camps and continuous excited argument. At least if there were significant differences among our teachers, I never learned about them. Differences among students were sometimes lively, and were argued out in meetings of student societies, but they never caused fundamental splits. When I went from Edinburgh to Oxford and became involved for the first time in active political discussion, I found bitter disagreements about politics among students and dons; but these reflected disagreements that were now general throughout the country. To take sides in the matter of the Spanish Civil War, for example, was to enter into a commitment in which all your political, social and moral thinking was involved. Politics were intensively divisive in the middle 1930s, and the divisions reached out into many other areas of thought. Still, I never encountered at Oxford any impassioned debate about the methods and principles of literary criticism such as that which I found in Chicago. Something of the kind, as I learned later, was going on at Cambridge between F. R. Leavis and his enemies, but at Oxford when I was there all literary discussion was pretty bland. Certainly, one would not see an Aristotelian critic cross the road rather than encounter a Platonist in the street, something I once saw happen in Chicago.

In Chicago I found a community excited by ideas in a way that I had not found either at Edinburgh or at Oxford, and I set this fact down now after all these years in the knowledge that it will outrage many in Britain who still believe in the provincial uncouthness of American, and especially Midwestern, universities. Not that I approved of everything at Chicago or much admired the American educational system. Nor was the intellectual excitement always of the most helpful kind. But it was there, and provided a climate in which my own intellectual life flourished.

My views on literature, and on the teaching of literature in universities, were radically shaken up during my first year at the University of Chicago. Though I had previously thought quite a bit about critical method and the problem of defining and locating literary value, I had never thought much about the technique of presenting literature to students. At Edinburgh Professor Grierson had given to first-year students the traditional magisterial survey of English literature from Anglo-Saxon times until the second half of the nineteenth century, providing information about books the great majority of which his audience had not read and in most cases would not read. It was a noble course, not so much because of its scope as because of the well-stocked, wide-ranging mind of the professor who gave it. The honours courses in the later years of the four-year course were essentially the same sort of thing on a much larger scale—a smaller period was discussed in much greater detail. Some lecturers marched pedantically through their material, and others—I remember George Kitchin especially—rambled on in easy talk full of witty asides, unprepared digressions, and bright thoughts that popped up as he talked. The poor students, who wanted from a lecture material they could give back in examinations, disliked him; but the good students, among whom I counted myself, found him fascinating. But nobody doubted that a *mélange* of history of ideas, biography of individual writers, summaries of plots of works and descriptions of their form and style, sporadic social history (when discussing, say, the literature of the age of Queen Anne), and intermittent value judgments phrased in a rather general and often impressionist manner, were what was required in a lecture on literature which was part of a "period course". And nobody doubted that the period course, or "survey course" as the Americans called it, was the backbone of university literature teaching, especially in teaching those who were not going on to be experts in the subject. Nobody doubted, further, the value of providing many students with *information about* literature they had not read and would not read.

Now this was precisely what I found being sharply challenged when I arrived at Chicago. The notion that information about literature that was not read by those to whom the information was given—and read in searching detail—was educationally useless and worse, positively corrupting, was entirely new to me. Though I had always loved literature as an art, and responded enthusiastically to its formal aspect, I had at the same time seen it as closely associated with history (both social history and the history of ideas): indeed, one of the reasons why I had decided to become an academic teacher of English literature was the sheer scope of the subject—it was liable to lead anywhere, and one could move out from discussing a writer or a particular work to consider historical, biographical, philosophical, political, sociological, psychological and linguistic questions. The study of literature led into the study of life in all its rich diversity. But at Chicago I found that McKeon had laid down the doctrine of *distinguishing disciplines*: the discipline of literary study was wholly different from the discipline of history and to consider a work as illustrating or illuminating the history of ideas when you were supposed to be presenting it as literature was a culpable confusion of disciplines. Crane followed McKeon enthusiastically on this point, in spite of his earlier achievements in the history of ideas. My "Platonic" preference for freely moving among the variety of human studies suggested by a literary work or a writer or a period thus stood condemned.

I do not propose here to give a history of my critical opinions (I have written enough about that elsewhere) but I am trying to describe something of the impact on me of the intellectual climate of the University of Chicago. I came to Chicago with a preference for the free-ranging discussion starting from literature of the kind I have briefly described; but I also had a passion for critical judgment. As an undergraduate at Edinburgh I had read *Towards Standards of Criticism*, a selection of critical articles from the short-lived periodical *The Calendar of Modern Letters*, chosen and introduced by F. R. Leavis with the intention of forcing the whole question of the nature of literary value and of literary judgment on to the reader's attention. This work influenced me more than anything else of Leavis I have ever read, not so much because of the actual value judgments pronounced (for I disagreed with many of them) but because of its challenge to produce them. At the age of twenty-three I had published a book of essays entitled *New Literary Values*, of which the first raised (however naïvely) the whole question of what literary value was and how it was established. So I was not hostile to the McKeon-Crane view that literary criticism needs a rigorous discipline of its own. But side by side with my desire for a sure method of evaluative literary judgment—and indeed operating as the actual cause of this desire— was my view that literature was valuable because it illuminated the human situation, not just because it produced patterns of meaning that were formally satisfying, though such patterns might well be means to the illuminative end. In my last year at Edinburgh University I had written an article for the undergraduate magazine, *The Student*, entitled with intolerable pretentiousness "Prolegomena to a Humanist Philosophy", in

which I developed a view of what I called the humanist value
of literature, and, though I would not now use the vocabulary
I employed then, it represents a view of literature from which I
have never essentially deviated.

So Chicago challenged me on two counts: it implicitly stig-
matised my fondness for wide-ranging literary discussion as a
confusion of disciplines, and it produced a discipline of literary
criticism which seemed to me wholly descriptive and not evaluative, and at the same time by-passing those elements in works
of literature in which, in my view, their value in the last
analysis resided. In its concern to find the unique principle of
organisation in the light of which a literary work could be
analysed it seemed to me to be moving further and further
away from the reasons which lay behind the appreciation of
literature on the part of even the most sensitive and experienced
of readers. It made comparative judgments almost impossible:
you either discovered the appropriate "organon" to employ
in analysing a work, or you didn't. If you didn't, you could
say nothing about it, and if you did, the descriptive analysis
that resulted had nothing to say about value, except perhaps
implicitly in the underlying assumption that what was analys-
able in that way was valuable. Further, such analysis required
a special technical training and the use of a special vocabulary
and turned literary criticism into a highly specialist activity,
engaged in competitively in order to impress fellow specialists.
This ran deeply counter to all that I had absorbed from both
Edinburgh and Oxford as well as to my own instincts as a
teacher. (Perhaps I should add that although my observations
on the McKeon-Crane method apply in some respects also to
the "New Criticism", being developed in America at the same
time by Cleanth Brooks and others, the Chicago School had
many points of basic difference from the New Criticism, as
was later made clear by Crane's attack on what he considered
Brooks's narrowness in his article "Cleanth Brooks and the
Bankruptcy of Critical Monism".)

In arguing about literature and literary criticism at Chicago

Sympathies

I sharpened my wits to a degree I do not think I have ever done elsewhere in a comparable period of time. And, although I remained suspicious, as I still do, of a purely specialist technical vocabulary for criticism, I learned to use critical terms more precisely and to eliminate from my writing elements of naïve impressionism which represented the final hang-over of my schoolboy reading of the early nineteenth-century essayists. In a sense I grew up. I can test this now quite easily by reading some of the things I wrote before this period, in which I nearly always find something to make me blush, and then reading something I wrote after this period, and though I may now think I was silly or wrong I am never made to blush in the same way. Yet, to repeat a point I have already made, my basic view of the nature and value of literature has never changed. I repeat this point, not out of pride, for it is surely nothing to boast about that one's basic view of anything in one's middle fifties is the same as it was when one was twenty, but to show that the cast of one's mind can be set at a very early age. Time and again, when I think I have followed an idea to an entirely new area of illumination I discover from some old notebook or in the pages of a forgotten article I had written years before that I had pursued exactly the same train of thought and reached exactly the same conclusion a long time ago.

Another thing that the intellectual atmosphere of Chicago brought out in me was my chameleon capacity. I have always had a certain gift for parody, but what I am talking about now, though it is related to parody, goes much further. I can enjoy putting myself into the frame of mind of a person who thinks in a way very different from the way in which I normally think and in that frame of mind producing arguments which he admires. I could not do this in a question of politics or ethics on which I had really strong feelings, but I could certainly do it as a kind of intellectual game in discussing a work of literature with, say, a Chicago School analyst, a myth-critic, a structural linguist, or a Lukács-type Marxist. Sometimes this can be more than a game, for one side of me will truly see and appreciate the point of view and the technique I am temporarily adopting. One has, after all, many selves. I remember once having a wonderful discussion, on a warm summer evening at Breadloaf, Vermont, with the Southern poet and critic Donald Davidson in which I developed *his* view of the importance of the Latin and Greek classics in education and of the social and educational decline which has taken place with the decline of the classics. It was also my view—but only up to a point. I am fully aware that with educational priorities as they are today it would be reactionary and obscurantist to insist on traditional drill in Latin grammar. Yet I love the classics; I was always good at them at school; and I can easily put myself in the position of the man who deplores their decline. With Davidson the problem was more complex, for his basic political and social attitudes were intensely uncongenial to me: yet by concentrating on one aspect of his educational views I was able to feel a full *rapport* with him and to argue vigorously on his side. So at Chicago I could produce in discussion with Crane an analysis of the *Religio Medici* which delighted him because it used his terms and employed his method, and I found intellectual satisfaction and excitement in doing this. But when I talked like this I knew that I was at best telling *a* truth not *the* truth and very often doing less than that, just having a satisfying intellectual game.

Except for a brief moment during my time at Oxford, when I was swept into left-wing politics by a desperation shared by most of my generation, I have never been a joiner. My instinct has always been to say at most "Yes, but—" to the programme of any school of thought. I retain sympathies for views I have abandoned. Though I have long been an agnostic, I have a passionate interest (literary, linguistic, historical, anthropological) in the Bible, and people are often puzzled when I write sympathetic articles on aspects of the Bible and turn out to be non-religious. To have a passion for the Bible and the Latin and Greek classics and at the same time to be on the left in politics is again often thought odd. I wrote a book on recent literature as a kind of relaxation between writing the chapters of my Oxford doctoral dissertation on English Bible translation; at Chicago I gave a seminar on James Joyce and at the same time was asked by the Oriental Institute to examine a thesis involving biblical Hebrew; I once translated some of the Hebrew poems of the Spanish Jewish poet Judah Halevi into modern Scots. I can understand—or I think I can—why intelligent Jews remain or become ultra-orthodox, why sensitive and thoughtful people convert to Catholicism, why some Americans are anti-British and some Britons are anti-American. One side of me can have splendid conversations with priests and rabbis and old-fashioned English classics masters. Another side joyfully addresses Humanist meetings, and exchanges ideas sympathetically with Marxists, atheists, and rebels of all kinds. I am both nostalgic for the past and impatient for the future. In all this I am doubtless like most other people, but I think my capacity for participation in intellectual discussion in different roles is perhaps unusual. One can agree with so many because they are all wrong. And of course because they are all partly right. It is, I think, my own intellectual eclecticism that allows me to take these different roles. It has nothing to do with cynicism—the reverse, if anything. I mean I think that it could be argued that there is an element of sentimentalism in my position. I feel for someone, I understand his intellectual and emotional standpoint, I can formulate arguments that will please him without violating my own integrity (though at the same time without telling the whole truth about my own position). Much of social intercourse, it seems to me (and a very great deal of intellectual intercourse) is based on such a pattern of behaviour.

But I must not exaggerate here. This role-taking represented a very small part of my intellectual life, at Chicago or at any other time. What I remember most vividly from my first year at Chicago was my being forced in controversy to define my own position much more carefully than I had ever done before. I recollect some pretty fierce arguments, one with a young disciple of Crane's who took what I said very personally and remained offended with me for a long time afterwards. For the most part, however, fierce argument and a gay social life went together. There were lots of parties. The younger members of the department could not afford to drink anything stronger than beer except on special celebrations (and somehow these seemed to turn up often). We would send round the corner for one of those enormous bottles of Fox beer and ask people in to talk. I have a particularly vivid recollection of a party given, I think, to celebrate the engagement of one of the younger instructors, at which a great deal of strong drink was consumed. It was on that occasion that George Williamson, the distinguished scholar and critic of seventeenth-century literature, a quiet man not usually given to riotous behaviour, mounted a chair, waved his handkerchief and exclaimed "Hurrah!" on hearing that a particularly difficult graduate student had been transferred from his supervision to mine. His nose started to bleed as a result of this unwonted excitement and he had to retire to a bedroom and lie down.

My teaching at the University of Chicago at this time consisted mostly of courses in the seventeenth century, and in the poetry and fiction of the twentieth century, as well as a general introductory course in drama and another on the same level in Shakespeare. It was, I think, my courses in the modern period that led to my being invited to give lectures on modern literature outside the university. There was a great hunger for instruction in modern literature, and a talk on the modern novel was always in demand. The Chicago Art Institute invited me to give a course of evening lectures on the modern English novel, and after I had delivered them the University of Chicago Press asked if they could publish them: thus was born the first book I published in America, *The Novel and the Modern World*. It was the money I received from the Art Institute for these lectures that paid the doctor's bill and the hospital fees at the birth of my son Alan in Chicago in February 1939.

Sympathies

I used to lecture all over the Middle West, not only at other universities but at women's clubs and cultural societies of different kinds. I had been told by a colleague always to ask for FAME ("fifty [dollars] and my expenses"), so these lectures provided a welcome supplement to my salary of $3,000 a year. I learned a lot about America from these travels. To talk to a women's club in Winnetka (just north of Chicago) or in a town in Iowa or Wisconsin was really to learn something about American society. A lunch-time talk to the Caxton Club, a society of wealthy book collectors who provided the only lunch I have ever attended at which a full bottle of Scotch or Bourbon whisky was set at every place, was a very different sort of experience and showed me the conspicuously culture-consuming American business male in action in an unforgettable way. Years later, when I was working at the British Embassy in Washington and did a great deal of speaking all over America as a public relations man for my country, I experienced a much greater variety of American audiences, but these belong to a later chapter.

Everybody now knows about American women's clubs, so I shall refrain from giving my amateur sociological account of them. My point is that I learned about them, as about so many aspects of America, from direct personal experience. And as I had no car I always went to these lectures by public transport, going up the North Shore from the Loop on the elevated railroad or travelling in old steam trains that puffed out into the neighbouring states. The rolling stock on these trains was often pretty ancient, sometimes with rather attractive interiors (bottle green plush seats in one case, I remember). This was before the aeroplane had ousted the railway as a significant form of public passenger transport, though the widespread ownership of cars had already begun its decline. There were still great crack trains in America then, running east to New York or west to California, and Chicago was a great railroad centre: all trains running west began from Chicago as the furthermost eastward point, and if you were travelling to the west coast from anywhere to the east of Chicago you had to

change there. Later on we were to have experience of the crack
trains, but those journeys to give lectures in Midwestern states
were generally made in local trains that stopped often and felt
as though they belonged to the nineteenth century. I liked them,
and I liked travelling in them. In Britain, where towns and
cities were established many centuries before the railway came,
the towns and cities took precedence, as it were, and forced
the railways to conceal themselves in cuttings or behind walls
or in tunnels underground when they came in. But in America,
where the railroad opened up so much of the country, it took
pride of place, and trains chugged cheerfully through Main
Street, the bell on the locomotive ringing to alert the inhabitants,
and the passengers were carried right through the very heart
of the town. I loved this sense of being carried through a living
landscape without being fenced off. Years later, in trying to
explain that sense of wanting to reach out and learn about
other people that one finds in the poetry of Walt Whitman, I
thought of those journeys in 1938 and 1939. Looking out from
an elevated train right into the rooms of houses (they never
seemed to draw their curtains) to see people in their daily
living; passing, separate yet right in the midst, through the
streets of small towns in Illinois, Wisconsin, Iowa or Indiana,
I had an almost yearning feeling of wanting to stop and find
out what it was like to be living in this room, shopping in this
street, standing on this corner; this was American life, these were
American people, going about their daily affairs wholly indepen-
dently of me; what did it mean to be *them*? I used to think of
Robert Louis Stevenson's poem, "From a Railway Carriage":

> Here is a child who clambers and scrambles,—
> All by himself and gathering brambles;
> Here is a tramp who stands and gazes;
> And there is the green for stringing the daisies!
> Here is a cart run away in the road
> Lumping along with man and load;
> And here is a mill and there is a river:
> Each a glimpse and gone for ever!

Sympathies

But the rural scenes from Stevenson's Victorian Scotland were very different from the bright, bustling, yet somehow featureless Midwestern towns through which my train took me. It was on these journeys that the Americanness of American life was most fully impressed upon me. The small towns of the Midwest, so new and spacious and lively and similar, both bustling and bare, were like nothing I had known in Britain or on the European continent. I felt that I wanted to know them, to understand them. Yet at the same time I felt that this kind of life, this sort of community, never was or could be mine. In spite of my almost desperate anxiety to know what it was like to be a small-town Midwesterner, I did not want to be one, I did not want to be content with their horizons, their memories, their hopes. As we entered on our first summer in America, the summer of 1938, and the weather grew hotter and the city stifled, both of us found our thoughts turning with deep nostalgia to Scotland. To be fascinated by a country, even to wish passionately to know exactly what it felt like to be born and bred and living in that country, did not mean, I now learned, that one would be content to live there.

I had left Edinburgh in 1934 to go to Oxford. This was success, this was adventure, and I had no time for homesickness. When I married a former fellow-student from Edinburgh in Oxford in 1937 we planned to go to France and live there for some time and were deflected from this by the invitation from Chicago. Everything was new and exciting and we never looked back. But suddenly, in that hot Chicago summer of 1938, we found ourselves reminiscing nostalgically together about Scottish places we knew. I wrote a poem in Scots about walking in the Pentland Hills. I had agreed to teach throughout the summer quarter at the University, because under the Chicago system if you taught all four quarters in one academic year (which meant taking a summer vacation of about five weeks instead of nearly four months) you got two consecutive quarters off, with pay, the following year. This meant that we could go back to Scotland for almost six months in early April

1939. It seemed an ideal plan, but neither of us anticipated the wave of nostalgia that hit us soon after the summer quarter had begun. It was quite specifically a nostalgia for Scotland. I did not pine for Oxford or London. But I wanted to walk again on the Pentlands, to re-visit the fishing villages of Fife, stroll again with my wife, as we had done before we married and she was working in the University Library at King's College, Aberdeen, over the Brig o' Balgownie, go back to the Northwest Highlands which we had explored as students. We used to pore over pictures of Scottish scenes in the *Scotsman* calendar. I remembered that R. L. Stevenson, too, had been an exile from Scotland in America and later in Samoa. I read him with new eyes and found uncanny parallels in our respective histories. For the first time I saw his remarkable unfinished novel *Weir of Hermiston* as an exile's novel, in which he sought and found a fictional means of embodying his feelings about the history and topography of his country. The dedication to that novel took on a new meaning:

> I saw rain falling and the rainbow drawn
> On Lammermuir. Hearkening I heard again
> In my precipitous city beaten bells
> Winnow the keen sea wind. . . .

Five years later, when I wrote my book on Stevenson in the scanty leisure afforded by a war job for the British Government in New York, this mood was still on me and led to what was perhaps my exaggeration of the element of nostalgia in Stevenson's later work. "His greatest achievment was to use nostalgia dramatically, to suppress all personal emotion while utilising that emotion in serious . . . fiction," I wrote towards the end of the final chapter. But I was writing about myself as much as about Stevenson.

Unlike my wife, who came from a Highland family, I could lay no claim to Scotland. I was not even born there, but in the north of England, though my parents settled there when I was so young that all my childhood memories are of Edinburgh. But in Chicago in the summer of 1938 I realised, to my own surprise, that it was my country and that I had a deep emotional feeling towards it. I have felt that ever since, though I have lived much more outside than inside Scotland. I must not exaggerate the change that this Chicago summer brought. Even as I write these words I remember feeling strongly about Scotland during my years in Oxford and attending Professor Fraser's course in Scottish Gaelic in order to make myself familiar with a part of Scotland's heritage that hitherto I had known little of. But the Chicago experience was different. It was then that I knew—and my recollection now is that the conviction came upon me suddenly—that whatever else I would do in the way of literary scholarship I would become an expert on Scottish literature and re-interpret it in my own way. Looking back now on my work on Burns, Scott, Stevenson, Hugh MacDiarmid, and eighteenth-century Scottish culture, I think I can say that I have in some degree realised that expectation. What I did not expect was that during the years when to return to Scotland as a professor was the height of my ambition, Scotland remained the one country of all those where I have studied or taught never to offer me a Chair or even to respond otherwise than negatively on those occasions when I was young and hopeful enough to apply for one when a vacancy was advertised.

CHAPTER FOUR

Farewell to Reverie

———◦◉◦———

THE University of Chicago toughened me both as literary critic and as scholar. I have mentioned how arguments with Ronald Crane and others both sharpened and sophisticated my critical discourse. But something more fundamental than a subtilising of methodology happened to me in the critical climate of Chicago. It was there that I finally shed the dreamily romantic view of poetry that I had cherished since childhood. I had been fond of poetry ever since I could remember, and written poetry regularly since I was nine years old. But though in my late teens I had developed that humanist view of literature as illuminating experience that I have already mentioned, somehow I never applied this in any serious way to poetry. I could enjoy for their vaguely haunting quality verses that I never bothered to construe literally. As a schoolboy I would carry Shelley around in my pocket as I walked on Blackford Hill, and I memorised Keats's "Ode to a Nightingale" (a poem which I still greatly admire, but for different reasons) because its lush musical languor seemed to me quintessentially poetic. I translated de Vigny's poem "Le Cor" for the school magazine, because the opening line

J'aime le son du cor, le soir, au fond des bois

seemed to me full of mystery and romance, and I laboured to put even more mystery and romance into my translation than existed in the original. I also translated a chorus of Euripides which I never fully understood, trying to make my rendering simply magical and suggestive. I loved Homer, and rolled his

Farewell to Reverie

Greek on my tongue, but I would have been hard put to it to explain why Homer was a great poet. I shared the nineteenth-century view of the eighteenth-century poets—the view I was taught at school, the view represented in Palgrave's *Golden Treasury*, on which I had been brought up—and believed that they were prosaic ancd mechanical.

There were paradoxes and contradictions involved. For I believed that poetry ought to be lucid as well as magical even though I did not always bother to follow the line of meaning. My first encounter with post-Georgian poetry left me annoyed and hostile. I had never read a single line of T. S. Eliot until my final year at Edinburgh University (1934), when I found "The Love Song of J. Alfred Prufrock" in an anthology of modern poetry I was given to review for *The Student*. I objected to what I considered the wanton unintelligibility and lack of form in some of the poems in this collection, but I praised "Prufrock" because I was moved by such lines as

> Shall I say, I have gone at dusk through narrow streets
> And watched the smoke that rises from the pipes
> Of lonely men in shirt-sleeves, leaning out of windows?

and the lines about the mermaids and the sea-girls at the end of the poem. In 1932 I won the Vans Dunlop Scholarship largely on the strength of an essay on modern poetry which explained exactly what was wrong with much of Eliot's poetry, though I had not yet read a single line of it. It was a purely theoretical analysis of the relation between overt meaning, associations and overtones, sound, and rhythm, which I later incorporated in my first published book, *The Place of Meaning in Poetry* (1935), written in my first months at Oxford as an entry for the Matthew Arnold Prize, for which I discovered, after having nearly finished the essay, that I was not eligible for I was not an Oxford graduate. I still have my copy of this book, filled with scribbled notes, objections, alterations, additions, sophistications, written after only a few months at Chicago.

Perhaps what happened at Chicago was only that I grew up, and the process would have happened wherever I was. The process had in fact got under way at Oxford, where I found students excited about Auden and reading Gerard Manley Hopkins. I was asked by the editors of the *New Oxford Outlook* (they were two young dons, Richard Crossman and Gilbert Highet, who have each won fame in different spheres since then) to write an article on recent poetry. I read everything that had so far been published by Auden, Spender, Day Lewis and MacNeice, and I followed them back to what Day Lewis claimed as their sources in his book *A Hope for Poetry*, round which my article was to be built. It was thus that I came to Hopkins, whom I found sometimes exciting, sometimes irritating. Some months afterwards, I read the volume of Hopkins's letters edited by C. C. Abbott, and wrote an essay entitled "Gerard Manley Hopkins and the Modern Poets", which became the first chapter in my collection of essays, *New Literary Values*, published in 1936. The other essays in this volume were on Wilfred Owen, whose poems I had discovered quite by accident in Edinburgh, Joyce's *Ulysses*, the stories of Katherine Mansfield, and three general subjects—"On Criticism", "The Judging of Contemporary Literature" and "Literature and Belief". *Ulysses* I read in my first term at Oxford and, in spite of its being very different from any kind of fiction I had previously known, I became an addict at once.

So when I left Oxford for Chicago some dents had already been made in the traditional romantic view of literature on which I had been brought up and which had so appealed to my youthful temperament. But though I knew Auden and his contemporaries, I did not know Eliot. I did not know the later Yeats. And I was ignorant of the mass of critical theory, even of such basic documents as Eliot's essays on "Tradition and the Individual Talent" and "The Metaphysical Poets", which underlay the modern movement in poetry. I was better equipped to handle the modern novel than modern poetry, if only because no body of modern theory about the novel had developed

Farewell to Reverie

comparable to the body of poetic theory that ran from T. E. Hulme, Pound, the Imagists and Eliot to the American "New Critics" who were now emerging. I worked out my own theory of the novel in 1936-37. I had become interested in Virginia Woolf as a result of a lecture on *Mrs Dalloway* given at Edinburgh University by the French critic and scholar of English literature Louis Cazamian. One of my Edinburgh fellow students had lent me Aldous Huxley's *Point Counter Point* as a daring modern work. So bit by bit I had built up some knowledge of and developed some ideas about modern English fiction before I went to Chicago. I have already mentioned that on my first critical encounter there with Ronald Crane I gave him my essay on the modern novel to read: this was the theory of the modern novel which I had worked out as a result of my reading especially of Joyce and Virginia Woolf.

Already at Edinburgh I had become aware of the revived interest in and admiration for the poetry of John Donne, for our professor, H. J. C. Grierson, was himself the distinguished editor of Donne and editor of the anthology of metaphysical poetry which Eliot reviewed in his famous essay on the metaphysical poets. But at first I had refused to join in the worship of Donne. In my first year I had written an essay attacking him as a verbal and intellectual exhibitionist whose baroque extravagance of word and thought ruled him out as a great poet, and my arguments must have carried some weight, for one of our lecturers took time off to argue at length with me to try to get me to see that I was wrong (it must be emphasised that this kind of relationship between teacher and student was virtually unknown at Edinburgh University in the early 1930s). But in my final year at Edinburgh my "special period" was the seventeenth century, and I got to know Donne well, and to admire tremendously the *Songs and Sonnets*. My second article for the *New Oxford Outlook* was on Donne.

During these immediately pre-Chicago years I had a somewhat negligent attitude to scholarship. I never bothered with precise references, set down all my quotations from memory, and was content to make large generalisations about the spirit of an age. In writing *The Place of Meaning in Poetry* I shockingly misquoted some lines from Tennyson and would have made an even worse blunder in a line from Racine if someone to whom I showed the proofs had not spotted it. I could rarely be bothered to check anything. A specific piece of research, written and presented as such, was of course another matter. At Oxford I attended lectures on bibliography, research method, the history of English studies, and similar topics of interest to research students and I found it all very interesting. Textual criticism I found particularly fascinating, and when Dover Wilson succeeded Grierson at Edinburgh and I became his assistant for a while, I eagerly read his and others' textual studies of Shakespeare. And in my own Oxford thesis on English Bible translation I checked references and stuck in footnotes with the best of them: indeed, I prided myself that if I wanted to I could be as pedantically scholarly as anybody, and when the book was eventually published I was delighted to hear the publishers complain that there were footnotes in a greater variety of languages than in any other book they had published. But this work was essentially a textual study, and I produced it in isolation from my other literary work. (I should add that I produced it in isolation from everybody. My supervisor at Oxford never saw a line of it nor did he give me any advice of any kind. I had a purely social relationship with him. This suited me. With the Bodleian Library at my disposal I did not feel that I needed anybody's help.)

My scholarly interests in my pre-Chicago days were thus divided from my critical interests. One of the first things that I learned in conversation with Crane—one of the most meticulous scholars who ever wrote—was the relevance of scholarship for critical and even more for historical judgment. My interest in relating literature to its social background, which developed in Oxford as a result of the political situation I have described, led me to make large pronouncements about the Age of Queen Anne, or Pope's relation to his audience, or the rise of bourgeois sentimentalism, and things of that sort, but Crane would always want to pin me down with a "who" and a "what" and a "where" and a "when". He hated historical generalisations, and he hated even more fiercely generalisations about the history of ideas (a field in which he was much interested). But the particularisation of his scholarship went hand in hand with what he liked to call a "dialectic". One could indeed construct a pattern descriptive of the history of ideas in a given period, but it had to have a thoroughly thought out intellectual structure anchored at the relevant points to the most specific examples. An excellent example of this is his now famous article on eighteenth-century criticism.

The emphasis on research in an American university produces an inevitable emphasis on accuracy and standardisation in citing references, and this is carried over into all critical writing and is not confined to scholarly theses. I was soon made to feel rather sloppy in comparison with the rigour of my American colleagues. This experience was a salutary check to my naturally impulsive way of writing. On one occasion I showed Crane an essay I had written on the structure of *Religio Medici*, which embodied ideas I had worked out in my course on "Bacon, Browne and Hobbes". I thought he might print it in *Studies in Philology*, of which he was then editor. He returned it after a considerable time, saying that he had read it attentively, that it contained some excellent ideas and that I would doubtless want to reflect further and work the whole think out more carefully. It had never occurred to him that it was anything other than a tentative first draft; whereas it had never occurred to me that an essay I wrote in the excitement of having just developed new ideas could be improved by re-writing. I never in fact re-wrote that essay, and to this day it remains unpublished.

While I benefited from the more rigorous and methodical writing habits of my Chicago colleagues, I cannot say that I altogether admired the standardisation and systemisation that went on (and goes on now to an even greater degree) in American graduate schools. Much useless pedantry is involved, and when, as so often happens, this is applied to trivial subjects of research or unintelligent exercises in a fashionable critical mode the result is pretty dead, even though it might have served its purpose in gaining its author a doctorate. But the problem of graduate studies in English in American universities, and increasingly in British universities, is a large one, and I do not propose to discuss it here. (I discuss it in some detail in the book on English studies in America which I wrote for the "Princeton Studies in Humanistic Scholarship" in 1962.)

The most significant part of my literary education at Chicago came from my being asked to give courses in Yeats, Joyce and Eliot (these were three different courses). They were either lecture courses for final-year students or seminars for graduates, and in either case it meant that I had to do a great deal of very careful reading both in the work of these authors and in recent criticism and scholarship. I have said that I did not know the later Yeats before I went to Chicago. This is not strictly true; I had reviewed for the Edinburgh University English Literature Society Yeats's volume entitled *The Winding Stair* when it came out in 1933. As I had no knowledge of Yeats's development and was quite unfamiliar with his characteristic imagery, and indeed knew only the anthologised poems from his early work, I was puzzled by these strange and complex poems, and I found "Byzantium" particularly haunting, though I had not the faintest idea what it was all about. The rhythms of such a line as "Shade more than man, more image than a shade" stuck in my mind, and emerged in a poem entitled "Spring in November" which I wrote in 1935 (and which appeared in *Poetry* in November 1938). But this was not knowing Yeats. Now for the first time I read through all his published poems and plays in chronological order; I read his prose; and I read the quite considerable body of criticism that had recently developed. I did the same for Eliot. I read Cleanth Brooks's *Modern Poetry and the Tradition* when it first appeared —my first experience of the "New Criticism"—and this in turn led me to a study of T. E. Hulme, the Imagists, and the tide of anti-romanticism that had toppled the view of poetry that underlay *The Golden Treasury*. I remained highly critical of this movement; I never joined those who acclaimed Eliot as the greatest poet of the century and the great renewer of the English poetic idiom; I retained serious reservations about "The Waste Land"; and I resented the fashionable jargon about poetry and paradox that was now being spouted on all sides. At the same time I was deeply influenced by what I read, and I realised that a tougher critical attitude and a more scrupulous critical method were required of me.

As for my own poetry, such as it is, I think it is fair to say that in spite of my pre-Chicago poetical views having been rooted in what might be called the Tennysonian tradition, it had already grown more astringent in tone in my Oxford days: I still like, for all its crudities, the poem entitled "Cosmogony" which I wrote in 1936 and which later appeared in *Poetry*. (It is in three stanzas, the first beginning "High up are the angels with best quality wings", the second beginning, "Down below are the devils with genuine horns", and the third, "Here is Mr L. Smith retail grocer".) This was a far cry from the long un-finished poem in Spenserian stanzas which I wrote in my last year at school, stanza after stanza of broody, self-indulgent melancholy in musical cadences. Yet I had also written great numbers of comic poems in my youth, I had written the words and music of two musical comedies produced by amateurs in 1929 and 1930 (when I was still at school), and had edited a home-made humorous magazine. Indeed, in those days I was, in the humblest possible way, an example of that divided sensibility that Eliot talked about, keeping my wit for comic poems and writing serious poetry unrelieved by wit. The kind of colloquial humour and music-hall liveliness that Auden intro-duced into his poetry impressed and influenced me when I was at Oxford. But I was still an elegiac romantic at heart. Perhaps I still am, but my Chicago experience forced on me a thorough re-examination of my poetic theory and practice, brought me firmly into the twentieth century and enabled me to see on the map how I had got there.

I continued to refuse to equate modernity with excellence and to accept the fashionable as good merely because it was fashionable. But whatever I did, from now on I had to put more systematic thought into it. Even as I write, I remember the last lines of "Spring in November" and recall the circumstances in which they were written. They seem now to have been prophetic. I was sitting by the window of my little study at the top of our family house in Edinburgh one sunny November day in 1935. It looked and felt like spring. Outside, the sunshine gilded everything with a hopeful brightness. I was moved to sudden, irrational happiness, the kind I used to enjoy in moments of rapt feeling when the external world seemed simply a vehicle for one's sensibility. Then I remembered what was going on in the world, especially in a Europe now increasingly dominated by Hitler. The last stanza ran:

> We may not trust our values to our sight;
> Cold sun can cauterize the world
> Deceptively. What, have you lost your soul?
> Black trees against blue sky bring no salvation.
> Pure and much stained (pure to the sight, yet stained)
> The world rolls round this morning.
> God, how our values roll themselves together
> Baffling the mind. Farewell to reverie.

There had indeed been too much reverie in my approach to literature. It was Chicago that finally exorcised it.

In Chicago I was confronted for the first time with literary criticism and scholarship as a great national industry, which has of course grown enormously since then, and I was not happy about it. And while one side of me continued to believe in the importance of determining and applying standards in judging literary works, and remained anxious to develop objective techniques of discrimination, another side of me regarded the whole thing as a game, which was all too easy to play. I had no doubt about my own judgments of major literary works:

virtually all my life I have admired and reread Shakespeare and continually found more in his plays to justify my view, which is the conventional one, that he is without doubt the greatest poet and dramatist Britain has ever produced. And I knew clearly why I preferred Yeats to Eliot and Joyce to Lawrence. (I saw Lawrence's greatness, I think, from the first time I read him, which was early in my stay in Chicago, but I have always considered his greatness marred by the intrusion of hysteria, nastiness, and irrelevant autobiographical elements. He irritated me profoundly. In the first edition of *The Novel and the Modern World* I had no chapter on Lawrence: I found that I could not write about him in a proper critical frame of mind. In a much revised edition produced in 1960 I finally got round to writing two chapters on him and to setting out as clearly as I could my views of his qualities and his limitations.) Minor writers, however, especially contemporary writers of some interest but doubtful permanent value, I found that I enjoyed writing about as an intellectual game. I could do it this way or that way, using the vocabulary of this school of criticism or of that, come down at the end on one side or another according to my mood or the degree of playfulness which overcame me. Except with pretentious rubbish hailed by reviewers as profound, which I felt it a moral duty to expose, I could never feel that stern obligation felt by F. R. Leavis to treat with total disdain everything that was not a hundred per cent up to standard in terms of integrity and maturity of feeling and perfection of craftsmanship.

I should add that I have never included any such lightweight criticism in my books; but in reviewing or in conversation I quite often engaged in it. The writers I have written about at length in books I have always been genuinely engaged with, having something positive and (I hope) original to say. America offered me many—perhaps too many—opportunities for "occasional" criticism, both written and oral. I slipped more and more into the regular critic's life. This was all the easier because my literary tastes are catholic. I can find something amusing or agreeable or even moving in books that I would not read twice, but which could be made the subject of an essay or a squib or a parody or simply a taking-off point for some general observations about life or letters. I am not claiming any great value for this kind of activity, and I don't want to be remembered by it. It was, I suppose, my form of sport. I have never been interested in physical sports or in games. Except for walking and fishing, I indulge in no physical exercise. I have never played cards, and it is the literal truth that I am not certain of the difference between clubs and spades (but I do recognise hearts and diamonds at once). I played chess as a child, but have hardly played at all since. My amusements are parasitic on my major interest; they are writing light essays or light verse. These are not activities much esteemed in modern America, so sometimes I disguised the light essays as serious reviews or articles. It was only when the *New Yorker*, at a time when it was starved for light verse and personal essays, discovered my talent for these sub-literary forms and encouraged me to write for them that my recreations came out into the open.

I find it hard to be certain of my own motives on this question. That literature was to be my profession—my serious, devoted, whole-hearted profession—I have had no doubt since childhood. At the same time, solemnity always provokes me to irreverence. Often, sitting on university committees or on other solemn bodies who behave as though their deliberations are of the utmost consequence for the fate of the universe, I find rising up within me an impulse to puncture the solemnity with a piece of deliberate levity. I remember once, when giving the "commencement address" at a small college in the Finger Lakes, I suddenly had as it were a God's-eye view of that little community of gowned students sitting in front of me with necks craned upwards as they hung on my words, and I saw the scene in relation to everything else in space and in time, and it seemed silly and comic and moving simultaneously. Fortunately, I went on with my address as though nothing had happened. Another experience which is perhaps relevant to this discussion happened in Oxford just after I had heard that I had been elected a Fellow of Balliol. I was twenty-three, and many years younger than the youngest Fellow of the College. I remember walking across the quad that warm summer evening and saying to myself, with an inward chuckle: "By God, I've *fooled* them!" And during the many years in which I have enjoyed (if that is the word) the title of "Professor" there have been occasions when it seemed ridiculous to me that I should be occupying a position with such a solemn and pretentious title. Though I am now in my late fifties, I sometimes find myself being surprised that I am grown up. I once mentioned to the late President Day of Cornell University that I thought there were two kinds of people: those who could not wait to grow up and those who could never quite believe it when they had grown up, and I shall never forget the grave bafflement with which he stared at me while trying to frame a reply.

I wrote many light-hearted critical essays in which I took up positions in order to try them out, as it were, rather than out of real conviction. But my genuine, committed criticism, in which I wrote as persuasively as I could exactly what I thought, and tried to find language that conveyed the precise qualities of the literary work under discussion and by doing so communicated a sense of the value as well as the nature of the work (what I call "loaded description", a critical technique I am now much more self-conscious about than I used to be)— even this I did with enjoyment and, relatively at least, with ease. I slipped into being a literary critic because it seemed so easy and natural to write literary criticism. But what I really wanted to be, for almost as long as I can remember, was a poet. I found that I wrote less and less poetry as I wrote more and more criticism. Then one day I realised that I had acquired a reputation as a critic and scholar when what I had always wanted was a reputation as a poet. I kept promising myself that soon I would find time to let my sensibility relax and brood so that I could devote myself more and more to writing poetry. Then the war came, leaving me trapped in America, and the mixture of nostalgia, frustration and anxiety that resulted led me to write poetry certainly, but damaged my style. Very little of the poetry that I contributed to *Poetry* during the war years now seems to me much good. The best had nothing to do with the war or myself: I think particularly of an oblique and tightly written sonnet, entitled "Ulysses' Library" which appeared in *Poetry* in January, 1941: it was an attempt to distil in a few lines the human meaning of the library scene in Joyce's *Ulysses*.

I started writing poetry again, after a gap, when I went to Cornell late in 1946. But this time I wrote not for *Poetry* but for the *New Yorker*. Not all of the poems of mine which the *New Yorker* published were light or comic: one of the most serious, and I am sure one of the best, poems I have ever written appeared in that magazine in June 1950. For once I managed to combine lightness of touch with absolute seriousness of purpose. The poem was called "Back in Time to Fix Lunch", and was about the "noontide repast" that (according to Milton) Eve promised to make for Adam when she returned from her first walk in the Garden alone. When she came back she was no longer the same Eve, and the promised lunch was never made or eaten. It was the most important uneaten lunch in history.

It was, then, my years in Chicago that committed me to criticism. And oddly enough, though my real passion was poetry, it was as a critic of fiction that I first made my reputation. I think this was because in wrestling with the nature and significance of *Ulysses* and its relation to earlier as well as to contemporary fiction, I really thought my way into the central problems of the modern novelist. At least, I think I did, and others were generous enough to agree. On the other hand, when I followed up *The Novel and the Modern World*, at the request of the publishers, with *Poetry and the Modern World*, I was writing a commissioned work, which did not arise out of any compelling original insight. I think the chapters on Yeats and on the early

Auden are good, and I stand by them today; but the book as a whole is more of an exposition for students than an utterance of my own deepest insights. I have consistently refused to revise it or bring it up to date, because to have the power I believe a book of that sort ought to have it would have to be re-thought out from the beginning, and so be quite another book. It was published in 1940 by the University of Chicago Press. Shortly afterwards the same publishers brought out my Oxford doctoral dissertation on sixteenth and seventeenth century Bible translation. I was keen to have this published, to show that I could produce meticulous scholarship as well as criticism, and the Press were very willing to do it, but they asked for a subsidy because of the very heavy cost of printing the Hebrew, Greek and other languages which were freely quoted. I had no money for this, but I was advised by a colleague that I should offer to do the book on modern poetry without any royalties—that is, give the Press all the rights for nothing—on condition that the Press would publish the book on Bible translation without charging me. The Press accepted the deal, which turned out to be highly advantageous for them and not at all for me. *Poetry and the Modern World* still sells, somewhat to my embarrassment, and the book on the Bible has recently been brought out by a new publisher in a new edition.

CHAPTER FIVE

Journeyings

———◦◦◦———

ONE dark, chilly morning in late March or early April,
1938—it cannot have been later than 5 a.m. and there
was as yet no trace of sunrise—the telephone rang in
our apartment in Blackstone Avenue, Chicago. The caller was
Napier Wilt, and the call was pre-arranged in order to get us
out of bed in time for us to make a very early start on our first
trip to the South. Wilt taught American literature at the University of Chicago, and was (and I hope still is, though he is
now retired) a gastronome, traveller, Negro-lover (yes, he loved
Negroes for being Negroes), theatre-lover, and collector of early
American glass, with an immense human curiosity about
people and things, especially in the literal and cultural by-ways
of the United States. He was a self-indulgent bachelor, and he
lived with his friend Bill McCullum, who was not an academic
but a civilian employee of the U.S. Army who had something
to do with food supplies, in the only apartment in his area that
was occupied by white people. He used to make epicurean
excursions on Sunday nights, exploring different foreign restaurants in Chicago, generally in the company of his fellow
Americanist Walter Blair and Blair's wife Carol, and often my
wife and I would be invited to accompany them on these
gourmandising excursions. We visited Polish, Czech, Hungarian, Turkish (I think) and Russian restaurants, each of
which had its own national clientele as well as the relatively
few curious outsiders. Generally Napier had cased the joint
before suggesting a group visit and had discovered the *specialité
de la maison*. It was often good, and it was always large.

66

The excursion to the South was in a sense an extension of these urban gastronomic trips. Napier talked of crawfish bisque and corn bread and hominy grits, but especially of crawfish bisque. He told us of the glories of Antoine's in New Orleans, of gulf shrimps and pompano en papillote. It was characteristic of him that he was as interested in basse cuisine as in haute, in peasant, petty bourgeois and upper bourgeois (which is as high as you can go in America) cookery. But of course he proffered other inducements too, geographical, sociological and historical. Not that we needed much persuading. He had worked out a precise budget, and told us exactly how much a ten-day trip would cost. The Blairs would come too, and we would all go in one car and share the running expenses. And as we wanted to get as far south as possible on the first day we would start before dawn. That is how we came to find ourselves emerging half-awake from our apartment building on that dark and chilly morning, to enter the waiting car with Napier at the wheel and the Blairs sitting in the back seat. Napier and Walter were to take turns driving: at that time I did not own a car and had never driven one in my life.

We were really sitting ducks for a couple of expert Americanists, two young innocents from Britain with only a few months experience of the United States making their first visit to the South, seeing for the first time the Mississippi, Spanish moss, "ante-bellum homes", to say nothing of Southerners, both unreconstructed white and oppressed black. We were happy to be sitting ducks. We wanted to see everything and learn about everything. We were the perfect audience for the two experts, drinking in the information provided and asking intelligent questions. Napier was a fluent talker and a devoted teacher; Walter had a slower and more ironic style, sometimes punctuating his colleague's eloquence with dry observations or sardonic cracks. They were excellent foils for each other.

We drove non-stop to Cairo, Illinois, which must be at least three hundred miles from Chicago. The only Cairo we had heard of up till then was in Egypt, and for the first time we began to see sense in the American custom, hitherto so ludicrous in our eyes, of saying "Rome, Italy" and "Paris, France". In the Midwest you have to say "Cairo, Egypt" if you want to make clear that that is the city you are talking about, although it is true that the Illinois city is locally pronounced "Kay-ro" —which might constitute a difference at least in the spoken language if one could be sure that the Egyptian city would not be similarly pronounced by many Illinoisians. There is Rome, New York, and Athens, Georgia, and York, Pennsylvania; there is also a Rome in Georgia, one Athens each in Alabama, Ohio, Tennessee and Texas, and Yorks in Alabama, Nebraska and North Dakota. I believe there is also a Cairo in Georgia. And so it goes. My memory of Cairo, Illinois (I have not visited it since) is of sunshine and warmth. We stopped briefly to stretch our legs, and as I got out of the car I was bathed in warmth and light and realised that we had journeyed from late winter into ripe spring while remaining in the same state.

I knew that America was large—after all we had travelled by train from New York to Chicago—but that Illinois alone contained such diversity of climate astonished me. Illinois is indeed a misleading state. Chicago is at its north-east corner and the state then spreads downwards (as it were) right into the south, with Missouri on its western side and Kentucky bordering it on the south-east. Cairo is about as far south in Illinois as you can get, and to me it felt as far from Chicago as Florida was. We were in the warm South now, and pushed on after a brief pause until we reached Memphis, Tennessee. We spent the night in a hotel there, and in unthinking obedience to a European impulse I put my shoes outside the bedroom door before retiring, so that they might be cleaned. To my surprise and annoyance, the next morning when I opened the door to collect them they were not there. I waited, thinking that the shoe-shine boy had not yet returned them but would do so soon, but no sign of shoe-shine boy or of shoes appeared. I rang down to the desk and told them that my shoes had disappeared, and the girl asked why on earth I had put them outside the door. It was then that it dawned on me that one is not expected to put one's shoes out to be cleaned in American hotels. The girl said, not very hopefully, that she would try and find out what had happened to them, and meanwhile I had to go down to breakfast in my socks. It eventually transpired that the bellboy had assumed that I had intended to throw the shoes out, and had therefore appropriated them. We persuaded him to return them, and compensated him by presenting him with a couple of bottles of California White Port.

How, it may be asked, was I in a position to make the bellboy such a presentation? It would never have happened had Tennessee not been a "dry" state, having decided to retain prohibition even after the repeal of the Prohibition Amendment in 1933. I was to be surprised at the number of states which stayed dry, and to suffer some bitter experiences as a result of my ignorance. Napier was anxious to show us how bootlegging worked, and what could be better than to use a totally dry state as a demonstration of American ingenuity? Napier had his contacts: we found throughout our trip that he was always darting off to look up an old friend, a Negro store-keeper, a small town newspaper-publisher, the owner of a roadside restaurant. In Memphis he found for us a really splendid character, a Negro giant who rejoiced in the appellation of "the King of Beale Street". He had an enormous liquor store in catacombs under Beale Street, and we were led down there through secret steps and passageways. There were shelves upon shelves of bottles, lit up by brilliant naked electric lights. We gazed in admiration, while the King chatted amiably about his large and diverse stock. He was pleased that we had come all the way from Great Britain to see him, and to mark his pleasure presented my wife and myself with two bottles. When we got back to our hotel room we scrutinised the labels and saw (to our disappointment) that the contents were described as California White Port. I can't remember where we got the corkscrew, but we did get one, and opened, and tasted, one of the bottles. The stuff was horrible—crude, sweet and sickly.

A Third World

We hastily corked the bottle up again and planned to secrete both bottles in the room before leaving. But the bellboy's disappointment at losing his new shoes gave us the opportunity to dispose of them. He bore them away, delighted, doubtless to sell them eventually at an extortionate price to some thirsty, innocent and, I hope, undiscriminating guest.

Southwards we sped, along the great Mississippi River, which at two points we crossed on a ferry. We saw bayous and river-boats and mud; we saw camellia, japonica (is the latter a red version of the former, or are they quite different shrubs?) and other colourful flowering shrubs that brightened the landscape, in contrast to the Spanish moss that hung gothically from the trees. We crossed the state of Mississippi from north to south, and somewhere in the course of that traverse we encountered the living Miss Haversham of Dickens's *Great Expectations*. That is to say, we found an elderly woman who had kept her dining-room table set with the family plate for decades, as Miss Haversham had left her wedding breakfast to acquire dust and cobwebs over the years. It was an "ante-bellum home" called, I think, 'Rosedown'. Impoverished English dukes may boast of having found a way of preserving their stately homes by showing them to tourists for a fee, but the American Southerners were there before them. Many a southern home was preserved as a museum which visitors could pay to enter. 'Rosedown' was set on a decayed estate, with forsaken gardens and overgrown paths and long neglected outbuildings. It started to rain as we arrived. Two aged sisters received us in the kitchen, where they lived, and told us about the history of the house. Their father had been a great Southern gentleman before the "war between the states" and had kept high style here. Look: we would see for ourselves. We were taken into a spacious dining room, of elegant proportions with an ornate ceiling, in which a large table lay set as for a dinner party for at least a dozen people. The lace table-cloth was thick with grime; dust lay visibly on the plates; the silver candlesticks and cutlery were tarnished; in a corner of the room water trickled gently from the ceiling on to a superb little eighteenth-century table. One of the ladies noticed the dripping, and said to her sister: "The water's dripping, honey, on the antique table". To which her sister quietly replied: "It always does, Eola, it always does". Eola then turned to us. "All these beautiful things our father collected," she said, embracing with a gesture the room and its contents. "And", she added with a cunning smile, "*we* have the use of them". We paid fifty cents each for this experience. As we left, I noticed the wall-paper in the dining room and the hall curling away from the top of the wall to hang hopelessly in sullen rolls.

That was the most direct lesson in the history of the South that we received on this trip. We passed on the road white share-croppers and Negro agricultural workers, and we saw the visible segregation in the living areas of black and white in the towns; but we had little personal human contact with the ordinary daily life of the Southerners. At Napier's insistence we sampled various wooden shacks of restaurants in small towns in Mississippi and Louisiana, but I have no very lively recollections of their gastronomic delights. I do remember, however, that at about eleven o'clock one morning, as we were driving through some tiny township in Louisiana, we passed a hut which advertised crawfish bisque and Napier insisted that we all go in and have a bowl. We knew that something was wrong as soon as it came; it was off, or high, or rancid, or something. The Blairs, my wife and I gave up after the first smell, protesting that it was inedible. But Napier, whose pride was involved, said that it was excellent, and spooned down his complete bowlful. We then rose and went out in the hot sun outside. Opposite, at the other side of the street facing an open patch of ground (or was it facing the river? this was more than thirty years ago) there was a bench, and Napier suggested that we sit there for a bit before continuing our journey. His large face was pale, and he kept mopping his forehead with his hand-kerchief. We sat in silence for a few minutes. Then Napier suddenly rose, dashed a few yards away, and vomited out the crawfish bisque. The matter was never referred to again by any of us; but I suspect now that the vomiting may have saved Napier's life.

That evening we reached New Orleans, and ate pompano at Antoine's, the only expensive and luxurious meal of our trip. The next day we walked in the Vieux Carré, the rectangle lying within the walls of the original city, admired the iron grille-work on balconies and in courtyards, looked through arches at *parterres* and fountains and statues, and wondered what on earth a city like this was doing in the United States of America, who after all bought it from France, with the whole state of Louisiana, in 1803. (That much I knew from my school history lessons.) It seemed as much Spanish as American to us, though of course the newer part of the city in the south-west (where we spent little time) was merely American. New Orleans had the sense of having a past, in the European sense, more than any American city we had so far been in: later, we were to have the same feeling about San Francisco. It was culturally and sociologically complex and puzzling—and fascinating. We only stayed a couple of days, only got a whiff of its intriguing atmosphere, a sense of something corrupt and abandoned and beautiful, like a poem of Baudelaire. I have never managed to get back to New Orleans since that spring of 1938; it lies in my mind, a haunting and disturbing memory, not quite real.

From New Orleans we travelled east, and peeped over the Florida border as far as the vacant-looking city of Pensacola. The Gulf of Mexico as we drove by this part of its northern shore seemed sad and quiet and washed out, like a permanent Sunday afternoon. We then turned north, and drove through Alabama, Tennessee and Kentucky, returning to Chicago on a chilly, windy, sunny day. The next day I lunched on the south side of Chicago with Guiseppe Borgese at an allegedly Hungarian restaurant called, oddly enough, 'Mothers'.

Our next American journey on any scale took place the following September, when we drove with Ged and Esther Bentley and their small boy (now Professor of English at the

University of Toronto) from Chicago to the west coast. Iowa, South Dakota, Wyoming, Idaho, Utah, Nevada, California: we must have covered well over two thousand miles, which to anyone from Britain is a long, long way. It was years later that I first read Sidney Lanier's sour comment on Walt Whitman: "Whitman's argument seems to be, that, because a prairie is wide, therefore debauchery is admirable, and because the Mississippi is long, therefore every American is God". (Which we can counter by citing Whitman's 1855 preface to *Leaves of Grass*: "The largeness of nature or the nation were monstrous without a corresponding largeness and generosity of the spirit of the citizen".) One can see what was troubling Lanier. Whitman does indeed appear to be seeing a moral dimension in America's largeness and at the same time to be reaching out to larger-than-life gestures of panoramic love that would provide an appropriate ethical equivalent to America's size and geographical diversity. My American journeys gave me some understanding of this, and indeed provided the starting point for the interest in Whitman which I later developed. There *is* a moral dimension in America's size. Looked at from Europe, the U.S.A. is just a country comparable to any other country, a nation-state with its government, good, bad or indifferent, and its policies, good, bad or indifferent. But when you have been in St Francisville, Louisiana, Cody, Wyoming and Winnemucca, Nevada; when you have experienced the Mississippi and its vastness, viewed incredulously the moon landscape of the Bad Lands of South Dakota, stood by the Great Salt Lake, encountered bears in Yellowstone Park, been humbled by the imposing beauty of the Grand Tetons; when you have crossed the dairy lands of Wisconsin and the great corn states of the Middle West, the cowboy country of Wyoming, and prowled around ghost towns and exhausted silver mines in the West—when, in short, you have experienced something of the astonishing human and physical variety of the country, you begin to realise what an extraordinary human feat it was even to *conceive* of this enormous geographical mass as a single

F 73

nation. It is true, of course, that the original thirteen colonies which first formed the United States represented only a fraction of the present United States, but the conception was there from the beginning, and the new states were taken in as they were pioneered and settled. The European tends to think of the federal government as the only real American government and the individual state governments as comic-opera assemblies of no national significance. But one of the many things my American journeyings taught me was that the individual states are real, each with its own history and economy and character, and that the astonishing thing is that the federal government has survived. The United States of America was a feat of the moral imagination, and though we laugh at American school-children saluting the flag daily and parroting formulas such as "one nation indivisible with liberty and justice for all" (there is no need to emphasise how ironical *that* sounds in Negro ears, not to go further afield), we must remember that this is a moral vision, and out of it the U.S.A. was born.

The U.S.A. was born in politico-moral rhetoric, and that is the other side of the medal. The level of political discourse among the Founding Fathers, in the Declaration of Independence, and even in the shrewd argumentation of the Federalist Papers, is remarkably abstract. The Founding Fathers were eighteenth-century gentlemen who believed in reason, they were men of the Enlightenment who believed in self-evident rational truths that would be immediately accepted by all men once they were formulated, and they also believed that such truths repeated in the highest-sounding terms represented the way to conduct political discussion. For them, as for Cicero and Quintilian, the justification of the rhetoric lay in the truth and wisdom of what they were seeking to express. But, for many interesting reasons, rationality declined as rhetoric flourished. In the nineteenth century and well into the twentieth American politicians became the greatest wind-bags in history. Eighteenth-century textbooks on rhetoric (notably that of the Scotsman Hugh Blair) remained popular right through the nineteenth century in America long after they had been forgotten by all but scholars and antiquaries in Britain. But this moral rhetoric, that blows through so much American history and accounts for so much self-righteousness in the conduct of American foreign policy, is (to come back to my original point) a legacy of the moral vision which brought this enormous and diverse collection of lands into a single, albeit federal, government. I am not now thinking so much of the spirit of the pioneers, the wagon trains crossing uncharted and difficult country, the mystique of the frontier, the lure of free land, "Go west young man" and all that, as of the simple yet profound act of imagination that first projected a united states of America.

It is not surprising that Americans are impatient with the squabbling little nations of Europe and their long history of mutual warfare. In a standard American school atlas, published in 1934, the description of Great Britain starts off with the announcement that its area "is 94,278 square miles, or a little less than that of Wyoming". The British reaction to that is summed up in the one funny line in the silly old film, "A Yank at Oxford". The brash young American, observing the Lilliputian British landscape from a British train, remarks to the old gentleman reading *The Times* opposite him that you could put the whole of Britain into the state of Texas. To which the old gentleman replies, briefly raising his head from his paper: "With what purpose?" Whitman thought that the purpose of America's bigness was to induce a moral response of extraordinary largeness, a new comprehensive humanity. And in spite of the tightly woven patterns of prejudice, discrimination, xenophobia and manic local patriotism with which America had long been riddled, something of Whitman's vision is deeply entrenched in the American outlook (and I think it can be argued that there is such a thing as "the American outlook" which cuts right across political differences). The conflict between states rights and the federal authority looks from Europe like a conflict between local reactionaries and national progressives, and indeed sometimes it is something like this.

But the emphasis on the *"pluribus"* in the national motto *"e pluribus unum"* is not always and necessarily reactionary. What makes the "one" so remarkable is that it is made up of the "many". I found the difference between American states and regions fascinating, and I have watched with a sadness that is perhaps romantic the steady *Gleichschaltung* of the whole country in terms of supermarkets, hotels, gas stations and suburban houses. Our cross-country trip in September, 1938 brought us to a much greater variety of hotels than you can now find in the United States. I remember a large, old wooden building in Minden, Nevada, which was comfortable in spite of having the now unspeakable un-American feature of only one bathroom-cum-lavatory on each floor, and on later trips I have stayed in small stuffy wooden hotels in little Midwestern towns which, though they were not the last word in comfort, had character, and an air of belonging to that particular place with its special geography and history. I don't think there are many of these now. Even the luxury hotels of New York and San Francisco had their own character, whereas now they are totally de-natured. I recently stayed at the Pittsburg Hilton, where I was attending a conference, and I found myself surrounded by the accoutrements, the gadgets, the atmosphere of the international hotel style which you can find in identical form in Tel Aviv, New Delhi and Hong Kong.

The tension between the regional and the central in the theory and practice of government has always interested me: it is one of the unsolved tensions of the liberal political imagination. In reaction against the cruelties of nineteenth century *laissez-faire*, with its assumptions that the private pursuit of wealth by individuals was the only recipe for social good and that the casualties of such a free-for-all represented the inevitable price to be paid for progress, men of good will of my generation came more and more to look to central government planning as the means of eradicating the cruelties wrought by free enterprise. In America, Roosevelt's New Deal imposed federal solutions on reactionary local vested interests, and such triumphs as the Tennessee Valley Authority seemed to proclaim clearly the road to both social justice and renewed prosperity. Let the central planning authorities examine the problem, assess the needs, and determine the programme. But we have now learned about the other side of central planning—the inevitable bureaucracy, the lack of human understanding, the ignoring of the realities of a local situation. During the Second World War, when oatmeal rationing was introduced in Britain, it was pointed out in the House of Commons by a Scottish member of Parliament that in the north-east of Scotland many farmers paid their labourers, at least in part, in oatmeal, and to ration it would thus disrupt the farming economy. The immediate reaction of the English members was ribald mirth at the mentioning of such a quaint local custom in an assembly that spoke for the whole nation. The recent rapid growth of Scottish and Welsh nationalism is a response to the centralisation of all British government in London and the unimaginative and often ignorant (though often well-meaning) behaviour of Ministers and civil servants with respect to Scottish and Welsh problems. Liberal thinkers brought up to believe that nationalism is bad (*vide* Hitler) and internationalism good found themselves faced with a dilemma: they believed in internationalism yet they felt that justice and humanity demanded some concession to the claims of nationalism within the British Isles. I should think that most informed people today believe that some sizeable degree of devolution in Scotland and Wales would be a good thing.

But the question of devolution is not really a question of nationalism. The complex apparatus of the modern state needs sensitive local antennae if it is not to turn into a heartless machine. But then again, the antennae must reach out to touch the real needs of the people and not reach only the vested interests of local business men and industrialists. The American system, with its state legislatures, and with its members of Congress much more locally based than British members of Parliament, much more sensitive to opinion back home and much more prone to go home on "fence mending" trips, is theoretically well equipped to balance the human needs of particular regions against the impersonality of a central government machine. In practice, of course, it is too often the local vested interests, the oil men or the building contractors and others with money enough to set up a powerful lobby, rather than the ordinary people of the region, who derive advantage from this system; in practice, too, state legislatures are prone to throw their weight around in such matters as removing "un-American" textbooks from the schools, for the small-town American politician is not as a rule a very enlightened or a very well-educated person. Nevertheless, there are local legislatures and there are channels open to Washington: it is not the system, but the way it is often used, that invites criticism.

Let other pens (as Jane Austen would say) dwell on the scenic glories of the American west, with its great national parks, its deserts and mountains and valleys. I am not trying to compete with the professional writers of travel books. We had originally intended to go first to San Francisco, and then drive south along the Pacific Coast to Los Angeles, to land up at Pasadena where Ged Bentley was to begin a year's work at the Huntington Library and I was to work there for a month. But when we got to Yosemite we found time pressing, so we turned south and made for Pasadena without visiting San Francisco, which my wife and I visited on our return journey, by train, a month later. I have not seen Pasadena since those quiet, warm weeks in September 1938, when we shared a large frame house with the Bentleys at what now seems a ridiculously small rent. I am told that it has greatly changed since, but at that time it was quite removed from Los Angeles and it had a rather pleasantly faded air, as though it were inhabited entirely by elderly meditative scholars, and its flowers and shrubs and trees, sub-tropical in colour and variety, provided a perfect setting for academic work. I clocked in every morning, with Ged Bentley, at the Huntington Library, lunched at the canteen there, and came home in the late afternoon. There were few other people working there at that time, and we had the library almost to ourselves. I was finishing my Oxford doctoral dissertation, the bulk of which had been written at the Bodleian, and the difference between the two libraries struck me forcibly. At the Bodleian, I always worked in "Duke Humphrey", the ancient part; I had a seat in a musty alcove which I occupied daily. At the Huntington I worked in a bright, air-conditioned stall, with a silent typewriter (provided by the library) and members of staff at my beck and call to look up and fetch me immediately anything I asked. I got through an enormous amount of work. Sometimes in the evening we would drive up Mount Wilson, which rose behind the town, and watch the sun set from the summit. We made several excursions to Los Angeles, which we thought messy and without real character, and one day (it must have been at the weekend, when we didn't work at the library) we drove up the Pacific coast to San Luis Obispo. We visited San Juan Capistrano, and I have a snapshot of my wife and myself smothered with pigeons there. But for me most of the time it was a scholarly interlude at Pasadena, and I look back on it after thirty-one years with affection. In recent years people who know Pasadena tell me that I must have imagined that quiet, sweet-smelling town that invited meditation. But that is how it lies in my mind, and I do not want ever to go back and confront that memory with what the town has become.

The first leg of our return trip was by train to San Francisco: we took the "Daylight", the crack Southern Pacific train which left Los Angeles in the morning and arrived in San Francisco in the evening. We boarded it at the little station of Glendale (which I am sure must now be totally swallowed up in Los Angeles) and the snapshot of my wife and myself standing in the station shows it as almost rustic in its smallness and emptiness. We travelled "coach", and sat in orange seats in an orange train. During the journey a white-coated vendor of candied fruits called "Aplets" (made from apples) and "Cotlets" (made from apricots) gave the passengers a little lecture about his wares and then perambulated the aisle shouting gently "Aplets, Cotlets". I had an impulse to add "Alive, alive-O", but I refrained. We also refrained from buying any, for our meagre finances had been stretched to the limit and we had to watch our pennies carefully.

We liked San Francisco, the steep streets, the cable cars, the Chinese quarter, the Golden Gate Bridge (which we walked across). We spent I think two days there, walking most of the time, before setting out on the long train journey back to Chicago. We had been given an introduction to Albert Bender by Sarah Schaffner and we rang him up from our hotel, to receive an invitation to tea. Bender had been born in Ireland of an immigrant Jewish family, but he had long lived in San Francisco where he had made his pile and become a generous patron of the arts. I don't quite know what I expected from my encounter with him—perhaps an offer to finance a literary review (at that time I nursed ambitions of founding and editing one) or some similar cultural gesture—but in fact we had a very quiet and uneventful tea in a hotel, with mild chat about this and that, and nothing more. Bender was an old man by then, and I remember seeing his death announced a few years later. That was the only time I ever availed myself of an introduction of that kind. On numerous subsequent occasions I have been told that I must look up X when I am in Y, and sometimes have had a note of introduction to X thrust into my hand. But partly shyness, partly pride, kept me from approaching X. I hate thrusting myself on people; I don't think that, except for close relations and very intimate friends, I have ever in my life called on anybody uninvited. This has prevented me from meeting many famous literary people, from whom I used sometimes to get indirect messages that they would be happy to see me if I cared to call and to whom I used frequently to get introductions from third parties.

As I say, it was as much pride as shyness. "If they really want to get in touch with me, they know where to find me," became more and more my attitude. I used to be astonished at American friends who used to call on writers they did not know and had never met because they wanted to be able to say they had met them. Both students and teachers used to do this frequently when they came to England, out of a kind of cultural curiosity as much as anything else. Of course there were (and are) always the genuine researchers who were doing serious work on a living writer, but they would generally write and make, as it were, a professional appointment. E. M. Forster was always very patient with such people when they came to see him in Cambridge. I wonder how many scores of times he had to answer prepared lists of questions about *A Passage to India*. I myself, in my humble way, have been on the receiving end of such pilgrimages more times than I can remember. If people are genuinely interested in what one has written, it can be pleasant and profitable enough to arrange a meeting and talk with them. But it is friends of friends of friends who claim personal acquaintance who can drive one up the wall. We were in all fourteen years in America before I returned permanently to Britain to an academic post at Cambridge. For some time in Cambridge I felt like Emerson's man who had made a better mousetrap: it seemed that every American academic in Britain, both student and professor, made a bee-line for our house. Of course we were always more than happy to see and entertain our many real American friends, but it was the distant acquaintances of friends, and even people who had not even the most indirect personal relationship with me, who turned up in great numbers. Americans themselves are so hospitable that we felt we must not let Britain down in our response. But sometimes we were desperate. I remember one early summer's day before we had acquired our house in Cambridgeshire and were still living in a tiny flat in Bateman Street, where the only entry to the dining-cum-living-room was through the kitchen, people turned up at half-hourly intervals from mid-morning. And they were not friends, but either acquaintances or less than that. We had given one group lunch and were in the process of giving another group tea when the telephone rang. My heart sank. It sank even further when the voice at the other end began with those familiar doom-laden words, "You don't know me, but . . ." However, the voice went on to say that its owner was at Cambridge station, and had promised X that he would look me up in Cambridge "and say hello", but unfortunately he had left himself too little time and was about to take a train out of the city. Would I forgive him for not coming along personally? "That's *quite* all right," I said fervently.

All this may sound very stand-offish and what the Americans call British. But I hasten to add that some of our dearest friends are American and they are welcome at any time, day or night, announced or unannounced. I am not talking about entertaining or putting up friends, which we enjoy. I am talking about the assumption that if one is, in however lowly a degree, a man of letters, one is considered by certain kinds of travelling American academics a legitimate object of sudden visitation. I suppose one ought to be flattered, but I can't help resenting it. Perhaps I am altogether too sensitive on these matters. My wife and I share another sensitivity of this kind: we abhor *general* invitations, such as "You must come and have dinner with us some time" or "When next you are in London (or whatever the city is) you must look us up". Such invitations are meaningless—the former variety especially so. We would not dream of taking anyone up on one, and we assume that we are not meant to.

This digression leads naturally to the subject of American friendliness and hospitality, about which so much has been written. I have already mentioned how kind my new colleagues were to my wife and myself when we first arrived in Chicago. But there is more to it than that. I have consistently found that where an American shares your interests and sympathies a very brief period of acquaintance will reveal this fact, so that the process of forming a real friendship is speeded up. It is as a rule a much longer business in Britain, though sometimes Britons meeting abroad can get to know each other well very quickly: I recall my first meeting with Asa Briggs, in the bar

of the Ritz Hotel in Hyderabad, India, and how in the course
of one evening a firm and lasting friendship was established.
Of course, moving in academic and literary circles in America,
as we did, we were bound to meet some congenial people. Yet
the fact remains that they revealed themselves as such much
more quickly than the same kind of person would have at home.
As for hospitality, the mutual entertaining of American academics probably embraces a larger circle than such entertaining
in Britain, but I have not found it essentially different. Entertaining of visitors is another matter, and here Americans as a
rule do put up a better show. But it is difficult to assess the
meaning—the moral meaning, one might almost say—of such
entertaining. In the case of a distinguished visitor, it may well
be mere lion-hunting. Sometimes one detects a kind of pride,
a showing off of Americanism, cordial hospitality combined
with insistent questioning of the visitor on how he likes "our
country". And if, as later I was regularly to do when I was
working at the British Embassy in Washington and doing a
lot of speaking throughout the country, one found oneself being
entertained at business men's clubs or in other non-academic
places, the instant cordiality of people to whom one was introduced was positively startling. "Glad to know you, Dave," a
total stranger would say, thrusting out his hand. He had not
caught my surname, and had no idea who I was, but he was
glad to know me and he called me (which none of my friends
and relations ever did) "Dave". Sometimes, when you imagined
you were the guest of honour and that the man talking to you
with what seemed like a mixture of admiration and affection
was relishing the chance of having made your acquaintance,
you would be devastated to hear him say: "What did you say
your name was? Will you spell that?" And you realised that
everything that had gone before had meant nothing, absolutely
nothing, a mere unearned and aimless friendliness. The cult
of "togetherness" lies deep in American history and sociology.
Loneliness is un-American (and some important nineteenth-
century American novelists were caught between their desire

for loneliness and their fear that the desire was a betrayal of the national ethos); spontaneous cordiality to all comers is the best way to avoid the discovery, unsupportable in a social context, of real differences of opinion.

I am talking of a middle-class America of fifteen to thirty years ago, and I know that in some respects my observations are now out-of-date. But this book is about my American years, and I record the scene as I knew it. Many things have changed since those years, not the least of the changes being the virtual disappearance of the passenger train. There were still crack trains in America in 1938, and though when we travelled from San Francisco to Chicago we sat up for three days and two nights (it is true that the seats did recline), we were not conscious of roughing it. We could not in those days afford a sleeper, but the coaches were comfortable, the restaurant-car was well provided, and the service was good. We returned to Chicago impoverished in purse, enriched in spirit, and sad and angry about the state of the world, for Chamberlain had just returned from Munich and I was one of those who thought (and still think) his deal with Hitler there a monstrous betrayal. I started my second year of teaching at the University of Chicago with all kinds of political apprehension, but more confident both of my own teaching skills and in my knowledge of America.

It was a half year really. I had two consecutive quarters off in 1939, so we were able to spend from March to September in Scotland. It worked out very nicely, for our first child was due to be born in Chicago in February. It was soon after my son's birth, in February 1939, when my wife was still at the Chicago Lying-in Hospital, that I went to the travel agent who operated in one of the university buildings and booked our passage from New York to Glasgow on the Anchor Line's newest passenger ship, the *Caledonia*.

I had another year and a half of my University of Chicago contract to fulfil, but it had already been made clear to me that, once I had got my Oxford doctorate (I was to submit my thesis there shortly after getting home), promotion and a permanent position were mine if I wanted them. But in fact we had no intention of staying longer in the United States than my original Chicago appointment called for. Not that we had come to dislike America or the University of Chicago. Our eighteen months there had been exciting and rewarding well beyond our hopes, but more and more we felt our roots on the other side of the Atlantic. I have already mentioned the wave of nostalgia for Scotland that unexpectedly overcame us in the summer of 1938; it never subsided; throughout all our subsequent stay in America, interesting and satisfying as it was in so many ways, we were aware of it. In February 1939 the idea of returning to Britain (especially Scotland, but I wanted to see Oxford and London again too) obsessed me, and when I had got our passages arranged I felt ridiculously happy. I was haunted by the possibility that war would break out and we would never be able to get back.

It was early in April when we set off. As a sudden gesture of joyous abandon I decided that we would fly from Chicago to New York, where we were to embark on the *Caledonia*. Civil flying was already establishing itself in the United States and elsewhere, and there were regular flights between the big cities. I had flown only once before, on a tiny plane that flew from Orkney to the Scottish mainland. We knew that there was a risk, because the plane might be cancelled or delayed by bad weather, but we arranged to board the ship at Boston (where it was due the day after leaving New York) if we were unable to reach New York in time. But everything went well, even though the runway was covered with snow when the United Airlines plane landed in Cleveland. It took off again without mishap; the stewardess served lunch and heated the baby's bottle; and we landed on time in Newark. The driver of the bus from Newark helpfully let us off at West Street, where we found a taxi to take us to pier 45, where the *Caledonia* was waiting. (We had sent our luggage straight to the ship by Railway Express.) The Glasgow accents of the crew sounded gloriously in our ears. We were shown our cabin, which looked comfortable and spacious. While my wife fed the baby, I went on deck and watched the afternoon April sunlight playing on the traffic of the North River and the buildings of Manhattan. The political and military anxieties of the world were temporarily washed away, and I was happy. When I returned to the cabin, I discovered that our Chicago friends Louis and Hazel Landa had sent us a bottle of sherry to the ship, as a "bon voyage" present. We summoned the steward for a corkscrew and glasses and toasted ourselves while Alan fell asleep in his carry-cot.

The *Caledonia* was more than half empty on this off-season run, and we more or less had the ship to ourselves, It was a relaxed, unhurried voyage, taking ten days from New York to Glasgow. Alan would lie in his carry-cot on deck while we sat in deck chairs or circumambulated the ship. As dusk fell I used to stand in the bow, as far forward as I could get, and watch the ship ploughing eastward. I remember our first sight of the green shores of Ireland, and finally the Clyde and Glasgow. My wife's father and sister were at the dockside, and off we all went to Queen Street station for the train to Edinburgh. We had a cup of abominable coffee at the station while waiting for the train. We had forgotten how bad British coffee could be, and were surprised that other people drank it with apparent satisfaction. Yes, American coffee was certainly better; and as for the American crack long-distance trains—well, they had their points, but here was the good old L.N.E.R. and all my childhood enthusiasm for railway travel suddenly surged back over me as we clambered into an empty third-class compartment. I went to the lavatory to put the baby's bottle in hot water, and the train started, acquiring as it gathered speed that rumbledy-stum rhythm that only British trains had and which I now knew was what I had missed in the sound of American trains.

CHAPTER SIX

Interlude for Explanation

———⟶◦◉◦⟵———

I HAVE mentioned my fear in 1938 that we might be caught in America by the outbreak of war and be unable to return home. But we did get home in April 1939, and after spending some weeks in Oxford putting the finishing touches to my doctoral dissertation I went up to Scotland where we had rented a cottage in Strathtay for the summer, and there we spent an idyllic four months—idyllic, that is, apart from the worry we shared with everybody else at the time about the growing threat of war. We were still in Scotland when war broke out, on 3 September 1939; we had booked our return to America months before on the *Cameronia*, due to sail from Glasgow on 6 September. At first I assumed that with Britain at war I would be expected to stay in the country, which in fact I preferred to do. But I was advised to consult an advisory office hastily set up in Glasgow, and when I went there from Edinburgh (where I now was) on Monday 4 September I was told quite definitely to return to my job in the United States, where I would be more useful (presumably in a public relations capacity). At the same time a cable arrived from the University of Chicago expressing the hope that I would be able to return across the Atlantic and urging me to come as soon as possible. I had no job in Britain, having re-signed my Balliol fellowship in 1937 in order to accept the Chicago offer, and I had contracted to teach at the University of Chicago for an initial period of three years. I was also not only broke but in debt, for our trip home had been expensive and I had not yet paid back all the debts I had incurred in the

87

year of my marriage. Yet the thought of leaving a Britain at war, leaving my parents and friends and relatives to undergo a fate which at that time was unpredictable yet seemed sure to be pretty grim, was highly distasteful to me. Soon after war broke out the *Athenia* was sunk, with considerable loss of life, and I assumed that no more passenger ships would be allowed to sail. The matter was decided for me: I would not return to America, even though Chicago expected me. But then I received a telegram telling me that the *Cameronia* would sail on the 5th, a day earlier than originally planned, and giving the time on which we had to be on board. No visitors would be allowed to see the passengers off. So the matter was now decided the other way, and we boarded the *Cameronia* at York Quay, Glasgow, under conditions of feverish secrecy. Workmen had started to paint the ship a dull grey.

So by mid-September 1939 we were in the United States again. American passengers on board cheered when we came in sight of the Statue of Liberty, but I remember saying, as one passenger exclaimed "home at last", "for me it is exile". My mood was very different from that in which I had first greeted New York almost exactly two years before. It simply never occurred to me to feel relieved at being safe, or even at having my wife and child out of the war zone. Perhaps it was silly, perhaps it was romantic, but I felt deprived at not being able to share in the life of wartime Britain. And, though in fact no alternative was open to me, I felt guilty. I have never purged that sense of guilt, and that I am writing these lines now is witness to that. It hung over me throughout my subsequent years in America, and it was one of the main forces that drove me to put every kind of pressure on my superiors at the British Embassy, Washington, where I was to have a wartime job, to get me back to Britain. I did not get back until November 1944, and I had the ironic satisfaction of spending some weeks in London when the flying bombs and the rockets were falling. That at least gave me some sense of sharing Britain's wartime experience.

Interlude for Explanation

I must not get things out of perspective. I was far from being in a state of permanent gloom during the war years in America. I had a great number of interesting and rewarding experiences. My family life was extremely happy. I had many good friends. But I had an obsessional anxiety to get hold of every shred of real news about what was actually happening at home, to learn what every detail of daily life was like both in bombed and unbombed areas. Later, when I was working at British Information Services in New York, I was to become an expert in wartime Britain and wrote many pamphlets about different aspects of it (with material supplied from London) for the enlightenment of the American public. That helped a bit, yet it was not the same as being there. My desire to be there—or to have been there—had nothing to do with any kind of heroism. I had no desire to leave my wife and children (our second child was born in December 1941, a few days before Pearl Harbour) and thought with agonising sympathy of soldiers and others who had to leave their wives for an indefinite period. I could not imagine a liveable life away from my wife for any length of time. But, paradoxically, at the same time I chafed at being confined to the safe shores of America and actually wrote to the British Consulate General in New York to volunteer my services for the British Merchant Navy, only to receive a polite reply from the lady in charge of volunteer services saying that I had better stay where I was.

It was impossible for civilians to get passage on a Transatlantic ship, unless of course they were government officials or were on some kind of official mission. There were aeroplane services for much of the war, both on the northern route from Montreal to Prestwick and on the longer southern route via the West Indies and the Azores, but these too were reserved for official personnel. Stranded British citizens listed their names at the nearest British Consulate. The Consul at Chicago had a list of a thousand, for most of whom nothing could be done. For all the interest and variety of my life in America in these years, I was overcome at regular intervals by a feeling of deep depression that I was trapped, I couldn't get out, I couldn't hop on a ship and pay a visit back home, I was condemned to strain my eyes peering across the Atlantic to try and find out what phrases like "Britain can take it" or "Their finest hour" really meant.

I think it was at the end of 1942 that the British Government announced a plan to repatriate stranded citizens abroad provided they undertook to do whatever form of service they were directed into on their return. One had to apply to the nearest British Consulate and make formal application for a return passage. By March 1943 I would be due for a second six months' leave from the university with pay, and perhaps if I could persuade the university to pay it me in a lump sum at the beginning of the period we could all go back to Britain and my wife and children would have a little capital to help them restart their lives there while I went into whatever war service I was assigned to. Accordingly, early in 1943 I duly filled in my application at the Chicago Consulate, undertaking to go into the armed services if so directed when I got back. I was then sent for a medical examination, and it turned out that the Chicago doctor who examined me, though some twenty years older than I, was a Scot who had attended the same school as I had in Edinburgh. I was passed fit for military service. During the preceding months I had been a member of a military training course that the Military Institute of the University of Chicago (a wartime phenomenon) had arranged, largely for younger members of the faculty who expected to be drafted imminently. For America too was now at war. The University granted me leave of absence for the duration (they had already extended indefinitely their original offer of a three-year position). I was also given my six months' holiday pay in advance. I was all set.

But all set for what? I began to realise some of the complexities of the situation when I received a letter from the office in New York that arranged passages for the repatriation scheme, explaining that since I wanted to take my whole family back with me I would have to wait until they could find accommodation for all of us, which would not be easy. Further correspondence made it clear that the wait would be indefinite. Jack Bennett, an Oxford don stranded in America at the beginning of the war (he is now professor of Mediaeval and Renaissance English at Cambridge) had for some time been working in British Information Services in New York, a pretty high-powered American arm of the Ministry of Information which had recently been developed on a larger and more complex scale out of the British Library of Information. He suggested that I come to New York and work at B.I.S., while waiting for passage. So to New York we went, and for a year I worked at B.I.S., writing pamphlets, answering innumerable inquiries about every aspect of British life, thought, history, geography, and present situation, some by letter and some by telephone, writing drafts of speeches for certain British officials in the United States, talking about Britain at war to all sorts of groups, in daily touch with the Ministry of Information by cable and with Washington by telex. At the end of the year we still had been found no passage. And the American draft caught up with me: I received the standard peremptory notice to report to my draft-board. I was now in despair of getting back to Britain through the repatriation scheme, and decided that on being inducted into the American Army I would apply for transfer to the British Army, which I was told could be done. Then the B.I.S. authorities got to know about my draft summons and decided that my services to British public relations in America were too valuable to lose. They got in touch with the British Embassy in Washington, who asked to see the pamphlets I had written. The result of this was that the Foreign Office gave authority to my appointment as Second Secretary at the British Embassy in Washington, whither we went in the early spring of 1944 and where, except for two periods of service in England, one at the Ministry of Information and one at the Foreign Office, I remained until June 1946.

This is all by way of background to explain what I was

doing in America during the war years. And—I must repeat this, for I have an Ancient Mariner compulsion to affirm it periodically—I still feel guilty at having been in America during the war, although in the circumstances I had no option. A few days before I wrote this I was with my mother in her flat in Edinburgh and we were talking about the new book by my son-in-law, Angus Calder, *The People's War,* a detailed study of life in wartime Britain. I remarked on the strange feeling one had on reading an account by someone who was not then born, or was only an infant, of events which were part of one's own experience. "How do *you* know?" my mother said, "You weren't there." She did not mean it unkindly in the least, but I was smitten as with an arrow; all my old feeling of guilt rose up and I was reduced to silence.

If anybody is curious to know what kind of pamphlets I was writing at B.I.S., he can find a unique collection of them at Yale University Library. My old friend Jim Osborn—we had been at Oxford together—was a senior research fellow at Yale, and he wrote to me while I was at B.I.S. asking, among other things, exactly what I was doing there. In answer to his question I collected copies of the pamphlets I had written and sent them off to him. These pamphlets were all, of course, anonymous, put out simply by British Information Services. But Jim decided that posterity ought to be able to know that I had written them, and presented them to the university library to be catalogued under my name. The longest of them, and the one that took the most work, was called *The Production and Distribution of Food in Wartime Britain,* and covered everything from a brief history of British agriculture to the latest scheme for milk distribution. It gave me some satisfaction, when I was home in 1944, to be able to explain to my friends and relations there the history of and the true reasons for the various rationing and distribution schemes which they knew about only from the consumer's end.

CHAPTER SEVEN

Moments of Unreality

A T midnight on 14 September 1940 I found myself pub-
crawling in Manhattan with William Clark, a Common-
wealth Fellow from Oxford who is now Director of
Information at the International Bank for Reconstruction and
Development. It was not, of course, a pub-crawl in the British
sense, since New York does not have pubs in the British sense.
We had several beers in different bars, a brandy each at the
Whaler Bar, and coffee and apple pie at some sort of drugstore.
I was killing time before catching a 3.00 a.m. train to Boston.
I had run into William (who was at the University of Chicago
with me) the previous evening with David Riesman, and after
talking at the Harvard Club we had gone to dinner with a Mrs
Sloss, whom I had never met and never heard of, but who,
I gathered, was wealthy and liked to meet bright young men
from Europe who were involved in literature and the arts.
We did not actually dine at Mrs Sloss's apartment, for she took
us out to dinner at a French restaurant, but we went back to
her apartment for brandy. I am certain of all this, because
from 1 January 1940 my wife and I have kept a diary in which
we have noted down, briefly and objectively, each day's events.

The invitation to dine with Mrs Sloss came via William
Clark, who evidently had a roving commission to bring in any
promising looking literary chaps he could find. William had a
real nose for patrons of the arts and was a highly successful
diner out. My recollection of this particular dinner is imprecise
but wholly agreeable, yet I remember too that I was in a vague
sense of puzzlement the whole evening because I did not quite

know where I was and why. That whole day had been odd. I was in New York attending the annual meeting of the recently founded English Institute, at which I was giving a paper, and that afternoon I had turned up to hear a paper on modern criticism by Allen Tate to find with astonishment that it was all about me: it was a carefully formulated attack on my recently published book *The Novel and the Modern World* which was held up as a brilliant but for that reason perverse and dangerous example of the bad left-wing positivist trend among certain modern critics. I think that Tate thought that I was an elderly Briton who had summed up a life of subversive critical thinking in this final literary testament. In fact, I had just turned twenty-eight and looked quite a bit younger. When I rose (as I felt I had to) from the audience after Tate had finished to defend my position and protest against what I considered to be certain misrepresentations of it, I enjoyed the gasp of surprise which went up from certain sections of the audience when they saw what I looked like. No real argument followed, to my disappointment, for I was cocksure and highly articulate and ready for a full-dress controversy, but Tate and I fought later in the columns of the *New Republic*. That exchange, however, came to an abrupt end when he found one of my contributions insulting and refused to continue. We made it up eventually, and had some very cordial moments in Minneapolis when I was visiting there in 1966.

The point I want to make about my discovery that a lecture by an important older poet and critic delivered to a distinguished academic audience turned out to be largely about myself is that the experience seemed strangely unreal. I didn't really believe it. I didn't say to myself, "There's glory for you", nor was I angry that I was being attacked. It was just another proof of the complete oddity of New York in September 1940. The previous evening I had gone with Jim Osborn to the New York World's Fair, a strange experience in the midst of a world at war: I had looked incredulously at the Royal Scot, that crack train of the London, Midland and Scottish Railway

94

that had been sent over as part of Britain's contribution. We drank a great deal of beer, and at one point found ourselves at a stall where, for fifty cents or perhaps it was a dollar, they printed any headlines you liked (in huge letters) on a real newspaper. That explains why I still have lying around in a box somewhere a New York newspaper with the enormous headlines

COPS WITH LIVE RATS HUNT DAICHES, OSBORN

We thought this was inordinately funny, and on the way back to Manhattan on the Long Island Railroad we periodically burst into peals of wild laughter as we re-read our comic invention.

So that midnight-to-3.00 a.m. pub-crawl in Manhattan on 14 September was part of a pattern of unreality that is still associated in my memory of those few days in New York. Mrs Sloss, live rats, Pennsylvania Station at three o'clock in the morning—how odd, how very odd. I had left my wife and small son at Port Clyde, Maine, where we were spending four weeks after a hot and sad Chicago summer, during which I had been teaching heavily in the University's summer quarter and we had read about the fall of France and the isolation of Britain as the lone fighter against a Hitler who now dominated almost all of Europe. The whole external world was becoming unbelievable. As the train chugged north to Boston, to arrive there at 7.25 in the morning, I felt curiously dissociated from objective reality. At Boston I changed stations and took the 8.40 train to Thomaston, Maine, where I arrived at 1.25 to find my wife and some friends waiting for me with a hired car to take us to Port Clyde. That was real; one's immediate personal relationships were real. It was not a particularly decent attitude; but in the summer and autumn of 1940 I often felt that only my wife, child and myself were real. The thought of having to leave my wife and child to enter military or other war service—a thought which was never far from my mind and which represented something I was determined to do—

caused me anguish. And I knew that it was only because I was safe and protected in America that I could afford the luxury of this emotional paradox.

No sudden change occurred in the atmosphere of the University of Chicago on the outbreak of the Second World War. It was only after Pearl Harbour and the consequent entry of America into the war that changes took place fast. Nevertheless, things were not really the same in 1940 as they had been in 1938. The most conspicuous difference was in the political atmosphere. The unity of the Left, the general Popular Front alliance of New Dealers, anti-fascists, Communists and fellow travellers, which had earlier reflected itself in cosy and even sentimental gestures of solidarity, was now broken. A whole section of the Left saw the war as an imperialist war and preached American isolation on high moral grounds. I found that my participation in left-wing meetings of students and others, which in 1938 had been so natural and agreeable, with everyone concentrating on the Spanish Civil War and on the fascist menace in general, was now much more difficult. I was suspect as a citizen of one of the contending nations. I remember attending a meeting on the near north side of Chicago and finding, to my embarrassment, that all the speakers concentrated on attacking imperialist Britain and nothing at all was said of Hitler. I had promised to speak, and when I did, at the end of the meeting, I found the audience impatient of my view —a view which seemed to me the only sensible one—that the faults of British governments in the past or even in the present did not alter the fact that a Hitler victory would be an appalling disaster for Britain, for Europe and for the world. I began to withdraw from meetings where politics were discussed. The arguments seemed so ridiculously theoretical, so miserably unrelated to the facts. I had got involved in such meetings in all sorts of casual ways, as happened to me so often during my years in Chicago. You dropped in to see a friend and he took you along, or you promised to talk to a student group and found that that group was going along to join forces with another group. These meetings generally went on late into the night. I remember once listening late at night to some highly doctrinaire argument about why Britain should not be supported and suddenly asking myself: "What am I doing here? Who are these people? Is this real?" And I left quietly.

In other quarters, however, I was regarded as an expert on Britain's part in the war because I came from Britain. I don't know how many times I was asked to lecture on "British writers and the war". Now I knew a great deal about British writers in the late 1930s, in what might be called the age of the Left Book Club. But all this had suddenly become old hat. I subscribed to *Horizon* and continued to read the *New Statesman* (in spite of the war and submarines, mail still came across the Atlantic, though the intervals between European posts were often long) and read whatever new British poetry and fiction I could lay my hands on; but I couldn't really speak for British writers and the war. I think that much of what I said in those many lectures on the subject that I gave in Chicago in 1940 and 1941 must have been invented. Or rather, I did not exactly invent material, but I extrapolated, projecting the Mass Observation movement of the late 1930s so as to explain the documentary writing found in *Penguin New Writing* ("The Way We Live Now", "Shaving Through the Blitz") and such things as John Strachey's *Digging for Mrs Miller*. When I talked eloquently about what was going on in the minds of young British writers in the first years of the war, I was just guessing. I see from my diary that in October and November of 1941 I gave a series of five weekly lectures at the Art Institute in Chicago on British Writers and the War, and that the titles of the individual lectures were: Attitudes and Arguments; Literary Periodicals; The Poets; The New Journalism; The Present Outlook. I remember that I was surprised to find myself having no difficulty in talking readily about a literary scene from which I was physically quite cut off. I didn't fully believe in what I was doing, it wasn't quite real. Yet, oddly enough, when I was back in Britain in 1944 and talked to all sorts of people and laid my hands on almost everything I could find in the bookshops, I found that what I learned confirmed what earlier I had only guessed. And in 1969, reading *The People's War* by Angus Calder (who was not born until 1942), I see that his researches yield a picture not unlike the one I was purveying to Chicago audiences in 1941. Much of the credit for my getting the picture more or less right must go to John Lehmann's *Penguin New Writing*, which I was able to get regularly for the whole span of its life. Its varied and unequal contents really did reflect with some accuracy what writers were doing and thinking and feeling.

Of course some British writers did get out to America in 1940 and 1941, as part of a cultural public relations exercise, and I generally met them when they came. But those curious islands of experience in which one met a poet at a party were less real than the books one read. I remember talking with Louis MacNeice in the office of *Poetry* (232 E. Erie Street— how well I knew that address, for I wrote poetry and criticism regularly for this magazine from 1938 right through the 1940s) in April 1940, and then going out with him to Northwestern University and listening to him reading his poetry there. Again, it seemed unreal. I have a haunting memory of a party ("in Henriques' home at Evanston" says my diary) later that evening when MacNeice read from his forthcoming book of poems:

> Goodbye, Winter,
> The days are getting longer,
> The tea-leaf in the teacup
> Is herald of a stranger. . . .

That stanza has never gone out of my mind since. Shortly afterwards I was sent for review the handsome little Cuala Press volume which MacNeice entitled *The Last Ditch* and I recognised the poem at once on the very first page. As I read it, the quiet, restrained, somewhat sad, rather deadpan voice of MacNeice reading it came at once into my mind. Only recently I woke up in the middle of the night with the words of that first stanza sounding in my mind, in MacNeice's accents. Yet at the time the poetry reading, the party in Evanston, the group of Northwestern University professors hanging on the quiet words of the British poet, seemed a curiously *unrelated* experience, a kind of oasis, something cut off from the normal patterns of living. The date was 4 April 1940: four days later the 'Phoney War' ended with the British Navy mining Norwegian waters in a vain attempt to stop Hitler's prompt invasion of Scandinavia.

We were pretty impecunious at this time. My University of Chicago salary of $3,000 had seemed a lot when I first accepted the offer in the autumn of 1937. But I still had an overdraft at my Oxford bank, for I had married on an overdraft, and our four months in Scotland in 1939 had set us further back financially. We lived pretty simply, but I never seemed to be able to get clear. On the morning of the day of the MacNeice party my diary records that I secured a loan of $150 from the University, to be paid off in instalments deducted from my monthly salary. (I should add that my salary was raised to $3,500 when I became Assistant Professor the following year, and that that was the highest salary I ever received at the University of Chicago. However, financial pressure was relieved when in 1942 I was awarded the $1,000 prize for the member of the faculty considered to be the most successful teacher of the year.) My financial problems meant that I could never turn down offers to speak or to do odd literary hack work if there was a fee involved. The result was that I became involved in some very odd experiences. Lecturing on the novel to a women's group called 'The Friends of American Writers' at six-monthly sessions between October 1940 and March 1941, I was paid $10 a time (in cash, on the spot), and it was not easily earned. The comment in my diary after the first lecture was "not a very bright lot". At my fourth lecture, according to the diary, "I lost my temper with a stupid and wealthy woman who rose to denounce Hemingway (on whom I was talking) as a dirty Red. I doubt now if I will continue this series." But in fact I carried on to the end. The session on 26 February was, I noted, "placid", and I had no comment to make on the final one a month later except to note with relief that it was the last.

On one occasion I accepted a commission, for a quite considerable fee, to help re-write an autobiography of some intrinsic interest written by a well-to-do Southern lady whose sense of style and structure left much to be desired. Week after week she would come to my office at the University and I would spend long sessions with her, sometimes myself re-writing whole chapters. At last the job was finished to our mutual satisfaction: I had helped her to make a coherent whole out of the book and she went off to submit it to a publisher (but I never heard of its being published). I then waited for the promised fee. Week after week went by, and it never came. And we really needed the money. My wife suggested that I should write the lady a polite note, and it was only then that I discovered that I had completely forgotten her name. I racked my brains, and the name would not come back. I knew the name of the street she lived in, but not the number, so that was not much help. Day after day went by and the name would not come back. I began to wonder whether the whole business had ever occurred and whether the lady really existed. We decided we would go through the Chicago telephone directory looking at every name where the address was the same street as the one this lady lived in. We spent hours on this, but to no avail. Then, weeks later, I suddenly woke up in the early hours of the morning with the name on my lips. I dashed to the telephone directory, identified the full name and address, and wrote it down there and then.

But then there was the question of the letter. It was a delicate business, asking for a fee from a lady who had verbally promised it months before but who appeared to have forgotten all about it. After meditating many formulas I decided to render an account in a wholly impersonal way. I took a blank sheet of paper, typed my name and address at the top, and underneath

I wrote: To Professional Services: $75 (or whatever the sum was). Two days later I received a cheque for the sum, with a most reproachful note from the lady asking whether it had been really necessary, in view of our pleasant personal relationship, to send her a formal bill. But I don't think I should ever have got the money if I had not.

A stranger experience was helping to put in order the recollections of a retired doctor who had spent some years as a patient in a mental institution and was still capable of behaving rather oddly. He had written up his experiences at the institution, including vivid accounts of his dreams. His manuscript was totally disorganised, but I am sure that it was of psychiatric if not of literary interest. The whole thing had a certain surrealistic quality which might have appealed to some publishers, and I thought it was worth trying to put it into some shape. It proved an impossible job. Every time I persuaded him that a certain section should be expanded or contracted and placed in a more logical order, he would take his manuscript away saying that he saw exactly what was to be done and would of course do it, only to return a week later with a totally new section and more dreams. Eventually I came to see that there was no point in any outsider interfering at all: whatever value the work had, derived from its being the spontaneous production of its author. His wife used sometimes to accompany him when he came to see me, being a bit nervous as to how he would behave. She finally invited me to their house to receive my cheque. It was luxuriously equipped with, I remember, a large open Steinway grand piano occupying a corner of the living-room. She rested on the piano to write my cheque, and there was a moment immediately afterwards when I thought something else was going to happen. But nothing did: I said good-bye and walked out of the room and have never seen either of them (or the manuscript) since.

These financial extras were important to us, and most of them were considerably more than the $10 per lecture I received from 'The Friends of American Writers'. By mid-1941 I could generally count on FAME for a lecture, but there were some notable exceptions to this, of which the most memorable was the first lecture I gave at the Caxton Club. Pasted into my diary at 20 December 1941 is the following elegantly printed notice:

THE CAXTON CLUB

On Saturday, December 20th, at the Tavern Club, 333 North Michigan Avenue, at 12.30 p.m. we shall gather for good fellowship. Our guest speaker, Prof. David Daiches of the English Department of the University of Chicago, will speak on *Some Aspects of Popular Scottish Song*. A native of Scotland, Prof. Daiches attended both Edinburgh and Oxford Universities. All members are urged to bring guests and to make reservations early. Eggnog will be served. The tax will be $1.50 per plate. Gaylord Donnelly, *Secretary*.

I spoke after lunch, and I had been very careful to drink no more than would stimulate without fuddling me. The all-male audience of amateur bibliophiles were themselves pretty stimulated by this time, and some were a bit fuddled. They behaved a bit like small boys who had escaped from the vigilance of their parents and schoolmasters. What they wanted from me was something bawdy, and, having been forewarned of this, I had chosen as my subject something that combined scholarship with bawdiness. I discussed bawdy Scottish songs from those in David Herd's collection to *The Merry Muses of Caledonia* and on to "The Ball of Kirriemuir". And, I'm afraid I must confess, I sang. I was encored and sang again. I have rarely had such an appreciative audience in my life. I interlarded my presentation of examples with learned discourse on problems of transmission and on the sociology of popular culture. The mixture could not have hit the taste of the audience more precisely. I was, in a very literal sense, a roaring success. For this performance I received what was for me at that time the genuinely princely fee of $100.

They came back to me the following December for a repeat (at the same fee). And so in my diary for 19 December 1942 the following printed invitation is pasted:

Moments of Unreality

On Saturday, December 19th, at the Tavern Club, 333 North Michigan Avenue, at 12.30 o'clock (noon, not midnight!), we shall gather for good fellowship. Our guest speaker on this festive occasion will be Professor David Daiches, who regaled us with delightful poems and stories at the Holiday Revels last year. His subject will be "The Underground Movement in European Folk Literature" . . .

They had wanted the mixture as before, but I could not bring myself to cover exactly the same ground as I had covered the previous year, so I talked on a kindred though not an identical subject. My recollection of the affair is thoroughly mixed up with that of the first occasion, so I cannot precisely differentiate the features of the 1942 revels. But that the audience was equally appreciative is made clear by the fact that eight years later, when the smoke of war had cleared away and I was professor at Cornell University, I received a cordial invitation from the secretary of the Caxton Club to speak at their annual "holiday revels" and to repeat my previous performances which, they said, still lived warmly in their memories. The fee this time was expenses plus $250. I had recently finished writing my book on Robert Burns, and I talked on "Wine, Women and Song in Eighteenth Century Scotland". I have no invitation pasted into my diary this time, but I have a note to the effect that the proceedings went on until 4.00 p.m. I remember being particularly impressed when Franklyn Snyder, the distinguished biographer of Burns and then President of Northwestern University, rolled about in his chair with mirth at my narrating an anecdote I had found in Henry Mackenzie's memoirs.

But this is a chapter about moments of unreality, and I have included the Caxton Club performances because the first of them at least was a complete holiday from the real world. This group of (for the most part) well-heeled book-lovers on the spree were temporarily inhabiting, as indeed I was too, a Land of Cockaigne. Thirteen days before, on 7 December 1941, the Japanese had invaded Pearl Harbour and America had entered the war.

A Third World

America's entry into the war of course changed many things.
Graduate students and younger colleagues slipped at a steadily
increasing speed into the Services, and older colleagues got
jobs in Washington. Teaching schedules were tightened up.
Military programmes were introduced into the University. And
eventually I myself, as I have recorded in the previous chapter,
landed up in a war job in Washington. Washington brought
its own moments of unreality, but before I move on to those
let me go back for a moment to a dull, rainy Sunday in March
1941. The bookseller Ben Abramson had brought Henry Miller
in to see me at our apartment in Chicago. It was one of those
sad, dark days when the air hung heavy in the atmosphere and
speech itself slowed down. Henry Miller informed me that the
the day before he had seen the words "God is Love" chalked
in large letters on a wooden shack in a derelict slum area on
Chicago's west side. He expressed great joy and wonder at this,
and that is all of his conversation that I can remember. That
same evening I dined with Somerset Maugham before he gave
a very indifferent public lecture, and he told me during dinner
that one of the main reasons for the fall of France was that
clerks in French post-offices had long made a habit of consistently short-changing people. They were a corrupt society, and
thus incapable of defending themselves against evil. It seemed
a highly over-simplified explanation to me, and rounded off
a thoroughly unreal day.

The two most unreal experiences in my life happened after
I had left Chicago. The first occurred in the spring of 1944,
when I was working at British Information Services in New
York. I was sent, at a moment's notice, to speak on British
naval policy to a church society in a New England town,
because the naval attaché, who was supposed to have gone, had
became suddenly ill (or had been suddenly recalled, or something) and I was supposed to have the gift of the gab and to
be able to absorb a brief quickly. I was met at the station by
the president of the society, an alcoholic evangelist, and his
friend, a Sunday-school teacher who believed that the whole

104

course of the war was written in the Pyramids and that Churchill
knew this. After my lecture the two of them took me to the
former's comfortable house some miles from the centre of the
town, sat me on a couch between them, with a bottle of Scotch
on a coffee table in front of the three of us, and took turns
pouring into my alternate ears the maddest observations I have
ever listened to. On one side came praise of John Alexander
Dowie, the early twentieth-century evangelist from Zion,
Illinois (who comes into Joyce's *Ulysses*), and praise for his
remarkable faith cures; expressions of admiration for the British
people who had known how to handle the natives in India
and who could show the Americans how to handle their uppity
niggers; virulently antisemitic remarks; tearful expressions of
the speaker's passionate love for little children; and exhorta-
tions to fill my glass with more "hooch". On the other side
came recitations of the prophecies of world history found in the
Pyramids. It was late, and I was very tired, and I listened to
these bizarre observations in exhausted amazement. They insisted on accompanying me back to the hotel where I was
spending the night, the president of the society driving me
there in his car and both coming into my bedroom, sitting on
the bed, and starting to talk again. The president pulled a half-
bottle of Scotch from his back pocket, collected some glasses
from the bathroom, and the whole procedure started again.
They eventually left about 2.00 a.m., but were back at 8.00
the next morning to see me off on the train to New York. When
I told the story later to my American friends they insisted that
there are no American characters really like that and suggested
that I had imagined the whole thing. But I know I didn't,
because I wrote it up as soon as I got home, and circulated it
as a minute to the senior staff of B.I.S.

The other experience occurred when I was in Washington.
The war was now over, but I stayed on at the British Embassy
as attaché in charge of educational and cultural affairs until
the early summer of 1946. In February 1946 I was asked to
speak to the Early Birds Breakfast Club of Washington on

Britain's economic position. I did a lot of official speaking on behalf of the Embassy at this time, and had been briefed on the economic situation, since Lord Keynes was preparing to lead a mission to the United States to discuss Britain's problems with the appropriate American officials and everybody at the Embassy was full of Britain's immediately post-war economic problems.

It was only after I had accepted the invitation that I realised I had committed myself to joining a hundred Washington business men at breakfast at 7.45 on a February morning. As I lived in Bethesda, seven miles out of town, this meant getting up at an unconscionably early hour. And, worse than that, it meant being intelligent and witty at an hour when I was normally quite unable to speak at all. I faced the prospect with misgiving, and I did some careful homework the evening before the event.

The Early Birds were a group of Washington executives who met every Tuesday morning for a sportive breakfast at the Willard Hotel. They only occasionally invited a speaker, preferring as a rule—or so I was informed by one of the members —to have fun with each other without the restraint imposed by an outsider. I found, however, that my presence did not prove to be much of a constraint. When I arrived at the room in the Willard Hotel where they always met, I found a scene reminiscent of what used to happen in my old school at Edinburgh when the teacher left the room; men were shouting, whooping, slapping each other on the back, pulling out each other's ties, and overturning chairs. The noise was deafening. I stood at the door quite unnoticed while pandemonium cheerfully reigned. Then, precisely at eight o'clock, the president produced a frying pan, which he struck with a mallet. A brief silence ensued, during which I was recognised and shown to my place at the head table, and then the assembled company broke into the following song (sung to the tune of a once popular song, "Let's All Sing Like the Birdies Sing"):

Moments of Unreality

This is the way Early Birdies sing,
    Tweet, tweet, tweet, tweet, tweet!
This is the way Early Birdies sing,
    "Give us something to eat!"
Bring on your ham and your eggs and toast
    And coffee, black or sweet,
For hungry are we as the birds in the tree:
    Tweet, tweet, tweet, tweet, tweet!

This is the way the rest of us sing,
    Oowah, Oowah, Oowah;
O Gosh! O Death, where is thy sting?
    Oowah, Oowah, Oowah;
O waiter, O waiter bring on the food,
    We're dying on our feet.
Let's finish the noise, be good little boys,
    And sit us down to eat.

I was given a copy of the words (from which the above is transcribed), and apparently I was expected to join in, but I hadn't the heart.

The impact of this ditty, sung full-throatedly by a hundred Washington business executives, on the half-awakened mind of my startled self can only be compared to what the sudden appearance of Mickey Mouse would have done to an audience of Athenians watching a play by Aeschylus. The statistics I had carefully memorised fell from me; my mind swam; I plunged into the breakfast that was set before me without any full consciousness of where I was or what I was doing.

During breakfast, which was eaten seriously and without undue noise, I slowly collected my faculties. I was feeling almost myself when, breakfast concluded, the secretary rose to read the minutes of the previous week's meeting. As he began the reading, all hell broke loose. Howls, boos and songs assailed him, and everybody started throwing pieces of bread about. Then somebody turned off all the lights. The secretary seemed to have been forewarned of this, for he immediately produced from under the table a miner's cap with lighted lamp attached, put it on, and finished reading the minutes by this light. This aroused a tremendous uproar, but the secretary went on reading steadily—though no-one could hear a word—and after much more bread-throwing and some miscellaneous disturbances the company quietened down and I was introduced.

In the course of my career as a university teacher and a wartime public-relations officer I have had many difficult speeches to make, but I have never found it harder to deliver an intelligent, well-informed address than I did on that February morning in 1946, surrounded by frolicking Washington business men. I summoned up every inch of will-power, reaching down to my very toe-nails, and by an effort that left me exhausted for days I managed to give a picture of Britain's economy before the war, the changes brought about by the war, and the current position. I *think* I held their attention, but I was so intent on mustering my own resources that I was hardly in a position to judge. At least they didn't throw bread while I was talking. Some of them even asked questions afterwards, but I cannot remember what I answered.

When the last question had been asked and (I hope) answered, decorum again broke down completely. The sign for this was the removal of the bibs (kids' affairs, but jumbo size) that everybody had donned at the beginning of the meal. While the members were taking these off and preparing to depart, they sang a song officially entitled "Closing Ode". It went to to the tune of one of the dwarfs' songs in "Snow White":

> Tweet, tweet! Tweet, tweet!
> We're perched upon our feet—
> We've had our food, we've had our fun—
> Tweet, tweet! Tweet, tweet!
> Now it will be a week
> Till once again we meet—
> So all together, Birds, let's sing:
> Tweet, tweet! Tweet, tweet!
>
> Heigh Ho! Heigh Ho!
> As off to work we go—
> We're all in step and full of pep
> Heigh Ho! Heigh Ho!

Are we downhearted? No!
We're off to make the dough—
Now all together, one more cheer:
Heigh Ho! Heigh Ho!

I went home and to bed for an hour, instead of going on to
my office at the British Embassy, as I had expected to do.
When I finally arrived at the Embassy, one of my colleagues
met me as I was going into the building and remarked that I
looked pale. I was standing on the steps in a chill February
wind, and I could think of no reply to make to his remark
except:

And this is why I sojourn here
  Alone and palely loitering,
Though the sedge is wither'd from the lake,
  And no birds sing.

CHAPTER EIGHT

I Represent my Country

———○◉○———

ON Friday 14 April 1944 I lunched with Desmond Harmsworth (now Lord Harmsworth) and Stanley Wilson at a French restaurant in Manhattan: Desmond stood a bottle of wine as he had just sold a portrait, and I stood Scotch whiskies all round as it was my last day at British Information Services. We were an odd trio, all of us Britons stranded in America by the war and doing our war jobs at B.I.S. Stanley was a fairly recent history graduate from a British university and I think had originally come to America on some sort of scholarship, but I confess that my memory is not clear on this. Desmond was a painter more distinguished than I then realised, and had led a remarkable international existence before coming to B.I.S. in 1940. The three of us worked in the information division, answering questions, producing pamphlets and information papers, and in general acting as public relations people for Britain at war. Both B.I.S. in New York and the British Embassy in Washington contained at that time many people who were not career diplomats or foreign service officers but who had found themselves representing their country in America in one way or another as a result of circumstances. Some of the people sent out from England to serve in one of the special wartime offices were oddities or misfits at home, who seem to have been sent to America as a last resort. Yet on the whole we were an able and efficient group, and because we did things less orthodoxly and almost always much more quickly than the regular career officers I think we achieved much more than regular Foreign Office men could have done on their own. It was the outsiders and amateurs in B.I.S. and at the Embassy that put life and energy into public relations and many other things. Isaiah Berlin's weekly political summaries had a brilliance that none of the established officers could emulate. Jack Bennett's academic thoroughness in rooting out information brought a new standard into international relations. Chaim Raphael's range of American contacts, from trade union leaders to novelists, was phenomenal. Charlie Campbell's contacts with the press (he was an Englishman long resident in America as a professional newspaperman in New Orleans) were of an order that no embassy press officer could normally achieve. And my own talks to American audiences were so much more vigorous, lively and knowledgeable than the routine stuff dealt out by embassy speakers that I was often embarrassed to be told so by the chairman after I had addressed a meeting. (I say this without false pride or false modesty: I had a way with American audiences, and the $1,000 teaching prize I won at the University of Chicago is some evidence for this.)

I first met Desmond Harmsworth at B.I.S. New York, in the information division on the 61st floor of Rockefeller Centre. I had no idea who he was. He was sitting writing with his jacket off and his shirtsleeves rolled up, and I noticed that he had tattooed designs on his arms. I took him for some rough British seaman stranded in New York by the loss of his ship and given a temporary job at B.I.S. while waiting for another. It did not take me long to realise my mistake, but I am still puzzled about those tattoos. I have never had the courage to ask him about them. Jack Bennett was head of the information division of B.I.S., having gone there in 1940 when he was stuck in America on arrival there en route back to Oxford from his native New Zealand. He and Eric Bentley had jointly called on me in Chicago in the summer of 1940, two stranded young English academics wondering what to do. Bentley was not the only Englishman who found himself in America during the war to decide to stay on permanently, but he is probably the most distinguished of those I knew who made this decision.

A Third World

I had enjoyed my year at B.I.S., frustrating though it had been in many ways, for I was continually but unavailingly expecting news that we had been found passage back to Britain. We had been unable to find a place to live in New York, but we had found a rather attractive, rather ramshackle furnished house in Chappaqua, N.Y., a pleasant little town in Westchester County a good hour from Manhattan by train. So for a year I was a commuter, rising at 7.00 a.m. and catching a train about 8.00 a.m. It was a strange sort of life, stranger really for my wife than for me, and certainly more arduous, for she was left alone with two young children from eight in the morning till at least seven at night. We had no car and our house was at the top of a hill quite a distance from the shops. Sometimes I had to stay late and did not get home until well after ten. I normally had to go in on Saturdays, and every so many weeks I had to take my turn at Sunday duty. I found it intolerable to lose two hours each day in travelling to and from work, so I devised a careful programme. On the journey *to* New York I would read the *New York Times*, bought at Chappaqua station, for fifteen minutes, and for the next forty-five minutes I would work through a couple of lessons (and the accompanying exercises) in a Gaelic grammar, for my nostalgia for Scotland was at that time taking the form of a determination finally to master Scottish Gaelic, at which I had made several earlier attempts. On the journey home I would read R. L. Stevenson, on whom I had contracted to write a book for New Directions. After six months of this programme, my reading and re-reading of Stevenson (and of his letters, biography, and other relevant material) had reached the point at which I felt I could begin to write the book. By dint of determined practice, I taught myself to write in the train in spite of the constant shaking movement, and changed my programme so that instead of doing Gaelic grammar I drafted parts of the Stevenson book. I had a great pad of foolscap-size yellow paper, and I would write on my knee. Much of the book was in fact written in the train in that way.

I Represent my Country

I left for Washington on 17 April 1944, leaving my wife
and the children in Chappaqua until I could find a place for
us all to live. We all walked down Mill River Road to Chappaqua Station, where I left for New York on the 5.52 p.m. train.
Then a train to Washington, where I arrived at 10.30 p.m. I
had never been in the city before. I was struck at once by how
much milder it was than in New York, and with the cherry
blossom out the impression was one of moving from a cold
northern climate to a gentle southern one. The Embassy had
got me a room in a little residential hotel not far away from
Massachusetts Avenue, where the conspicuous red brick Embassy building was (and is) situated. "A small monastic room,
but sufficient," my diary notes. The next morning I walked
up Massachusetts Avenue to the Embassy, found my way to
the Information Office in the annex, and after some formalities
I was admitted and shown round. I had never been in an
embassy before. To come in now in what for me seemed the
exalted rank of Second Secretary was a curiously *literary* experience. First, second and third secretaries proliferate in late
Victorian and early twentieth-century fiction (isn't it Maugham
who has a tale called "The Third Secretary's Story"?), and
were associated in my mind with well-born young men who,
through family influence, got exciting but not taxing jobs in
Istanbul or Petersburg. It was a bit disenchanting to find that
I was to work in the hastily built temporary annex, which had
none of the splendour of the main building, but I did have the
luxury of a room to myself ("Somewhat bare," my diary notes,
"but it does have a leather easy chair for visitors"). But the
most exciting thing was to be given the day's telegrams to read.
I realised that I was to be on the circulation list of most of the
telegrams that went in and out of the Embassy. I cannot do
better than quote my diary again: "Most exciting behind-the-
scenes stuff (Churchill to Halifax and vice-versa, Eden to
Halifax, etc., etc.). One certainly is at the *centre* of things here."
During my two years in Washington I never lost that innocent
sense of excitement at being at the centre of things. Washington

was at that time the political centre of the alliance against Hitler, and anything of any international significance came through the Embassy in one way or another.

My work during the first year at the Embassy was very mixed: it included looking after the "fifty visitors" scheme, a scheme to send representative Americans to England to see for themselves what the country at war was really like. This involved getting transportation for them, through the air attaché, on R.A.F. Transport Command planes from Montreal to Prestwick, while the Ministry of Information found them "luxury hotel" accommodation in London. One of my other jobs was to write a weekly summary and evaluation of German broadcasts to the outside world, which were monitored in New York and sent to me hour by hour on teletype. Once a gentleman called Mr Remmie Arnold, who made cheap fountain pens and was head of an organisation called the American War Dads, asked if the British would find him transportation to go to England and visit the American boys there. I was suspicious of his organisation, but asked the military attaché to find out about it: he reported that it was an important and influential organisation of fathers of American soldiers fighting in Europe and elsewhere, and recommended that Mr Arnold be encouraged. (I suspected then and believe now that this was an exaggerated view of the organisation's significance: it has since disappeared without a trace. But of course I had to accept the military attaché's evaluation.) So Mr Arnold was flown by R.A.F.T.C. from Montreal to Prestwick and thence to London, and before he left he sent me a box of twenty of his cheap fountain pens. I was a bit taken aback at this, and thought that I should return the pens, but on consulting colleagues I was told that I had better just hang on to them, since I had received them after and not before the Embassy had made its decision and so it couldn't be regarded as bribery. The pens wrote quite well while they lasted, but they lasted a very short time. I gave most of them away, many of them to friends in England and Scotland where I was to go within a couple of months.

I Represent my Country

At the Information Office I did not have much contact with the regular Embassy officials, but after a year, when I was put in charge of educational and cultural affairs and moved from the annex to the Embassy proper, I found myself working in the midst of the professionals, with Michael Wright, then Head of Chancery, as my boss. I even came in contact with the Ambassador, Lord Halifax, and on one occasion addressed in the Embassy a group of American school-teachers on the British educational system as a substitute for Halifax himself (a former President of the Board of Education) when he decided he just did not know enough about the subject. He was in the chair, and I gave the talk he was supposed to give; it included a brief history of the English educational system which led him to remark to me afterwards that now for the first time he understood what the Education Act that he had introduced was all about.

I was always puzzled by Lord Halifax's reputation as an Ambassador who could really make contact with the Americans. I found his speeches stuffy and pedestrian, like those of most of the professional British diplomats in America at that time. Some Embassy speakers traded heavily on conservative Americans' admiration for high-toned British country life and blended a somewhat blurred aristocratic image with a sentimental flavouring combining Mrs Miniver with Mr Chips (though this was not Halifax's way). I could not bring myself to like Lord Halifax: I found him cold, dull and not really very bright. But he did his best. Shortly after I had come to the Embassy he invited my wife and myself, as newcomers, to a formal Embassy lunch. We had just moved from a fine house we had temporarily rented in Chevy Chase Parkway to a tiny house in Bestheda, Maryland, a good seven miles from the Embassy, requiring a journey in two different buses. We miscalculated the amount of time required, and arrived late. The other guests had been for some time sitting on the verandah sipping tomato juice. On our apologetic arrival we were offered sherry or tomato juice, and only after we had both taken sherry did we notice that everybody else was drinking tomato juice. We then went in to lunch. My wife, as the newcomer, was seated next to the Ambassador; I had sitting on my right (for the sexes were uneven in number and could not be regularly alternated) an ex-R.A.F. pilot who had lost a leg in the Battle of Britain and had now been given some unexacting job in Washington. The first course was a huge mushroom omelette, served on a silver salver. My wife, on the Ambassador's right, was served first. Imagining that this was the main course (for this was wartime, and everybody knew about British austerity during the war) she helped herself to a substantial portion. The other guests and the host and hostess were then served, and took a tiny little square of the omelette. My wife was shaken to see that she had taken so much more than she had evidently been expected to take. When the omelette came round to me, it was already clear what the situation was, and I took a large helping to keep my wife in countenance. We then discovered that the main course was roast lamb, which we had no real appetite for.

But worse was to follow. When fresh fruit was handed round, I took a pear. I noticed that the Ambassador also chose a pear. I said to myself that there were many ways of eating a pear and I would eat mine exactly as the Ambassador ate his. So I watched him, and imitated him. He peeled the whole pear before cutting it, and I did likewise. Then he seized a peeled half and sliced it down the middle. I too seized a peeled half of my pear, but it was wet and slippery and slipped out of my hand with considerable momentum to hit the wall before falling on to the floor and sliding under the table. Nobody at the table took the least notice of this, but a uniformed and knee-breeched attendant dived under the table to retrieve and remove the offending portion of fruit. As he did so, the R.A.F. man next to me bent down to try to assist, and in the process he got his wooden leg jammed against the leg of the table. I had to help him to extricate himself. It was a nightmare experience. All this time my wife was calmly discussing

Trollope with the Ambassador. She reported later that he repeated the word "Trollope" a couple of times and then, as though suddenly struck by the thought that it was a dubious word to use in talking to a lady, abruptly changed the subject.

After lunch we were taken to the drawing-room where Lady Halifax arranged everybody in couples (different from the grouping at table) and then, as soon as any couple got really involved in conversation, systematically broke the couple up and formed a new pattern. She herself sat by each guest for anything from three to six minutes. The whole process was mechanical in the extreme, and prevented any genuine conversation. We were glad to get away.

The liveliest and most idiosyncratic of the regular diplomats in Washington was Jock (Sir John) Balfour, who came to Washington as Minister from the Moscow Embassy in 1945. He had the most extraordinary habit of removing his clothes as he talked. On Fridays a group of us used to meet with him in his office to comment on the draft of the weekly political summary which Isaiah Berlin had prepared and which was cabled to London later in the day. Berlin's draft was always witty and well-informed, but everybody present was welcome to suggest alterations or additions. Balfour presided over these discussions, and at an early stage in the proceedings he would remove his shoes. Then he would take off his socks. Later on, it would be the turn of his jacket and waistcoat, and after that came the tie. It would end with his sitting on the desk barefoot in his braces, and I always had the feeling that if the meeting had gone on a bit longer he would have taken his trousers off.

Isaiah Berlin became a legend during his Washington days. He had been briefly at the Moscow Embassy (he speaks perfect Russian) where he had known Jock Balfour; the two often spoke in Russian together at the Washington Embassy. Isaiah was another displaced academic, whom I had known at Oxford. His famous speed of utterance used to fascinate and puzzle the Americans. Once a senator called at his office to ask him his views on some problem. Isaiah let out a torrent of words in reply. The senator listened in stupefaction, then replied: "Thank you very much, Mr Berlin, but the fact is that I haven't understood more than one word in ten". To which Isaiah replied (and the reader must imagine this tumbling out at furious speed): "One-word-in-ten one-word-in-ten that's-a-very-good-beginning very-good a-little-practice a-little-practice and then you'll get one-word-in-nine then-one-in-eight then-one-in-seven and-so-on-until-you-understand-everything a-very-good-beginning-indeed".

But the best Berlin story, which has long been legendary, concerns the confusion between him and the American composer Irving Berlin. I cannot vouch for the absolute accuracy of all the details of the version we got from London at the Embassy, but the main facts are certainly true. It seems that Winston Churchill was enchanted by the wit and gossipy liveliness of Berlin's weekly political summaries (which gave an account of the week's political trends in America) and gave instructions that the next time he was back in England on leave or for any other purpose he was to be invited to lunch. His conscientious secretary, noticing in the press that "Mr I. Berlin" had recently arrived in London from the United States and was staying at the Savoy (I think he must have been one of our fifty visitors), despatched an invitation to lunch to Mr Berlin at the Savoy, and Churchill prepared to meet the admired sender of the weekly political summary. Irving Berlin —for it was he, not Isaiah, who had arrived from America and was staying at the Savoy—duly arrived at Downing Street for lunch. There were no other guests, only Mr and Mrs Churchill and Mr Berlin. At the very beginning Churchill was taken aback by his guest's accent, and wondered how he could have acquired such a Brooklynesque accent in Washington so quickly. Irving Berlin, however, who took it as absolutely a matter of course that the Prime Minister should invite him to lunch in the middle of a war, was not aware of any uneasiness on his host's part. Becoming more and more bewildered as the conversation went on, Churchill sought to bring his guest down to essential matters by raising some important question of current American politics. Berlin replied: "I'm afraid I'm not interested in politics, Mr Prime Minister". At this point Churchill realised that something was very wrong, but he could not figure out what. To test his guest further he asked him: "Mr Berlin, what do you yourself like best of the pieces you have recently sent over to us?" (He was referring, of course, to the weekly political summaries, each one of which was a work of art.) "Oh, it was a little number called *Kissing my Baby Good-night*" (or some such title) Berlin cheerfully replied. Then Churchill knew he had got the wrong man, but, as he had never heard of Irving Berlin, he had no idea who his guest really was. It is said that at this point Mrs Churchill guessed the true identity of their guest, but history is silent on the conversation between that point and Mr Berlin's departure. It is recorded, however, that Irving Berlin never suspected at any time, either during or after the lunch, that he was not the man the Churchills had intended to invite.

Berlin's flair for political gossip, which so enchanted Churchill, was said to have been assisted by his habit of attending diplomatic cocktail parties (in which Washington abounded) and drinking only plain water, disguised as gin, while those he spoke to got ever more loquacious over their Martinis. I cannot vouch for the truth of this, but I do know that even at Oxford Isaiah had a reputation for witty gossip: in Auden's verse testament which concludes *Letters from Iceland* the poet leaves "To Isaiah Berlin, a saucer of milk".

Of the professionals in the diplomatic service, I found George Middleton the most intelligent and the most sympathetic: he came to Washington as Second Secretary about the same time as I did and became First Secretary the following year, after I had moved to Chancery to be in charge of educational and cultural affairs, so that then I saw quite a bit of him. Donald Maclean, later to become so notorious, was there too, and though I never got to know him well, my work brought me into occasional contact with him. I remember him wearing a spotted bow tie, rather dapper, with a slightly weary air. All the cables I wrote had to be approved by one of the established diplomatic people at the Embassy, and I remember once bringing a long cable to the Ministry of Education to Maclean for his O.K. (He was not normally the man to do this, but Middleton, who generally did it, was on leave.) He had evidently not heard that the Board of Education had become the Ministry of Education, though he knew that Ellen Wilkinson was in charge. (This was after the General Election of 1945.) When he saw the cable beginning "For the Minister of Education", he said gently, "For Madame la Présidente, don't you mean?" I had to point out to him that she was indeed a Minister and not president of a board. It is the only sentence that I can distinctly recall him saying.

After the war ended I had to deal with the enormous number of inquiries which came to the Embassy about the possibility of Americans studying in England under the "G.I. Bill of Rights". We got some extraordinary requests. G.I.s wanted to attend schools of ballroom dancing, cookery schools and scores of institutions I had never heard of. As I had to certify them as respectable before the Veterans Administration would authorise the money to enable the G.I. to attend, this meant referring many inquiries to London. I soon became something of an expert on the marginal educational institutions of England, but I am afraid that I have forgotten all I learned on the subject. The real trouble was the enormous backlog of Americans wanting to attend British universities, which had been closed to them throughout the war. With our own ex-servicemen flooding back, British universities were bursting at the seams, and it was just not possible to accept more than a tiny trickle of Americans. Pressure to accept more mounted steadily, and it was as a result of this that the compromise of British Universities Summer Schools, intended mainly for Americans, was devised. These still survive. The other permanent fruit of my educational and cultural activities at the Washington Embassy was the exchange of school-teachers between Britain and America. I worked out the general principles in many discussions with the U.S. Office of Education before discussing the details with Edith Ford of the English-Speaking Union in London in November 1945. (I was in London then for the opening and founding conference of UNESCO, or UNECO as it was at first, the S (for "Scientific") being added at this conference.) Later, Edith Ford, a woman of tremendous energy who was capable of crushing any obstacles to a scheme she had set her heart on, came to Washington and helped to sort out the American end and to select the first batch of American teachers.

My work at the Embassy Information Office was more varied than the work on the educational and cultural side. One of the problems that troubled us information people was the prospects for Anglo-American relations in what we called "stage 2", that is, after the war was over in Europe but was still going on in the East. Few Americans realised that the British were involved at all in the Japanese war, and the security people forbade us to release figures. (There was a constant fight between us and the security people, who often forbade us to issue information that was public knowledge and sometimes had actually appeared in the press. I formed the view that they were pretty stupid.) I remember once a minute came on to my desk dealing with this problem. It began: "Prior to the present world conflagration . . ." I changed this opening to "Before this war" and in the space for comments at the bottom I wrote: "In a war we are said to be fighting for the preservation of civilisation, I see no reason why the author of this minute should not be deemed to be on the side of the enemy". It subsequently turned out that the minute had been written by a very high personage indeed at the Foreign Office, and I was ticked off, albeit mildly, by my boss, Harold Butler. (Harold Butler, Minister in charge of information at the Embassy, remained a rather distant figure to us all. I never saw him doing very much. Isaiah Berlin used to say that he spent his time pouring cold oil on troubled waters.)

In both my informational and my educational and cultural

capacities I did quite a lot of speaking, which I rather enjoyed. But sometimes there were embarrassing moments. I always had a good time dealing with the anti-British left and with stock spirit-of-1776 haters of Britain as aristocratic and reactionary. The conservative pro-British could be more difficult. Once, addressing a meeting of the Lions Club in Baltimore, I was told with pride by the president over a pre-meeting drink in the bar of the hotel where the meeting was held that his branch of the Lions was racially pure and refused membership to Jews. I asked simply, "Why?", and he at once sensed my lack of rapport with him, changing his tune very suddenly to say: "Well you see, there just don't happen to be any Jews living around here". After the 1945 victory of the Labour Party there were groups in Washington who simply could not credit that the British had rejected Churchill: Americans themselves have an unfortunate habit of giving peace-time political office to successful or reputedly successful war leaders. Many thought that Britain was going communist. I rather enjoyed speaking to audiences who were disturbed about this, laying out the social and economic history of Britain in modern times and putting the Labour Government's policies in perspective.

I was much in demand to speak to Scottish societies, on St Andrew's Day or Burns Night. Some of these occasions were awful. Guests rigged out in every conceivable kind of tartanry but with no knowledge whatsoever of Scotland, its history and problems, arrived to hear vaguely sentimental oratory and were upset if they got something else. I remember once talking to a "Scottish" audience about problems and developments in modern Scotland, to be told by the chairman afterwards that the audience were all patriotic Americans who did not want to get involved in the details of Scottish affairs. Once I addressed the Clan Macfarlane Society in an eastern town, to find on my arrival that there were no Macfarlanes there at all, though everybody, male and female, wore the Macfarlane tartan. It turned out to have been a friendly society founded in the nineteenth century by a small number of Macfarlanes none of whom now survived. As I had prepared what I considered a rather winning introduction on the history and geography of the Macfarlane country, I had to change my speech rather suddenly when I discovered the realities of the situation. Once I shocked a Washington St Andrew's Society audience by beginning my speech (before which a florid singer had sung some bad sentimental songs about Scotland): "You have been hearing about the wee hoose amang the heather. I should now like to talk about its lavatory facilities", and went on to talk about housing in modern Scotland. Once my fellow guest at a Burns Night dinner in Washington was General Eisenhower: I was the principal speaker, and the General merely made a few pleasant remarks about Scotland. He was extremely agreeable, told me that he had never heard such a magnificent speech, and invited me to visit him in Culzean Castle, apartments in which the Scottish people had recently presented to him. I never in fact took him up on the invitation.

The only distinguished military or naval figure I met in Washington was Admiral of the Fleet Lord Keyes. This was in August 1944 when I was at the Information Office. Harold Butler was out of Washington, and by a chapter of accidents I happened to be the senior representative of the Ministry of Information in Washington at that time. Since Lord Keyes was doing some public speaking in various places across the American continent, and British Information Services in New York were responsible for seeing that he was well taken care of while fulfilling his speaking engagements, I was asked to meet him, representing B.I.S., on his arrival at Washington station from New York. He spent a few days in Washington to confer with both British and American naval authorities there.

As I was leaving the Embassy to go to the station the finance-and-establishment officer thrust a five-dollar bill into my hand with some muttered remarks about "incidental expenses" and "pocket money". "The Admiral may need it," he added, and went off before I could demand any further explanation. My general impression was that I was to give the money to the Admiral. To be sure, it was a ludicrously small sum, even for pocket money, but I knew that all the Admiral's expenses were being taken care of and that he would have nothing to do with the payment of his railway fares or hotel bills, or anything of that sort. And besides, were not British sea dogs supposed to be Spartan in their habits? I reflected on this, as I decided to do my duty in sailor-like fashion and refrain from idle speculation.

When I arrived at the station I found that the Embassy's naval attaché had arrived before me and had thoughtfully made inquiries about the spot on the platform where the Pullman car in which Lord Keyes had a reservation would come to a stop. He had been given the approximate reservation, and there he, together with an assortment of British and American naval commanders, captains and admirals, and a solitary Wren, had taken their stance in a spruce, disciplined row. I joined them, at the end of the line, feeling a little out of it without any uniform and trying hard to stand erect and look sailor-like.

The train drew slowly in. Without changing our positions, we all peered respectfully into the Pullman car that came to rest alongside us, but could see no sign of Lord Keyes. Suddenly, the naval attaché saw a man in a white uniform about to descend the steps of the next car. He pointed discreetly, and we all moved sideways, like crabs—evidently in such circumstances one does not turn round smartly and march—until we found ourselves, still in the same row, facing the Admiral. As he came down the steps, everybody saluted—everybody, that is except me. I was a civilian, and, what was more, I had no hat, so I could not even give a civilian gesture of respect. I thought of touching my forelock, but apart from being in some doubt as to whether I possessed such a thing, I felt the idea was too rustic, and immediately abandoned it. After some rapid and muddled thinking, I was surprised to find myself waving at the Admiral familiarly. He did not return my gesture.

I Represent my Country

Lord Keyes was taken in hand at once by the naval attaché, and we were all introduced. My turn came last and I was presented with the laconic description "British Information". When we had emerged from the station, though, the naval attaché took his leave and so did each of the others—again with a fine display of brisk salutes—and I was left with the Admiral, with the responsibility of getting him to his hotel and, presumably, of seeing to it that he had pocket money. It turned out to be easy enough to get a taxi and accompany him in it to the hotel door, but I was still doubtful as to what to do about the five-dollar bill. I kept it clutched in my left hand as we drove along, and I did not use it to pay the taxi-driver when we alighted.

I helped Lord Keyes to check in, saw him to the door of his room, asked if there was anything I could do for him, and received a cheerful assurance that everything was all right. We shook hands, and after I withdrew my right hand, I took the five-dollar bill from my left hand and thrust it at the Admiral, saying, "This is for you, sir. You might need a little spare change". I felt horribly embarrassed. He looked startled, but he took the bill, almost mechanically, and I retreated hastily towards the elevator.

When the Admiral's discussions in Washington were over, it was my job to collect him at his hotel and see him on to his train. On arriving with him at the station that day, I again found the naval attaché and a noble collection of brass and the one attractive Wren, drawn up in front of the coach ("car", as the Americans say) where Lord Keyes had his reservation. The Admiral and the naval attaché and the porters with the luggage and I went into the car. There was some fussing about the Admiral's seat—the naval attaché did not think it sufficiently comfortable, or dignified, or something of the sort—but eventually everything was arranged to everybody's satisfaction, and Lord Keyes descended from the car to the platform to take an official farewell. The attaché and I followed him out and joined the line of officers, and everybody except me saluted. This time

I had thought out my behaviour carefully beforehand, and I bowed slightly, the way high government officials do when they meet distinguished foreign visitors at an airport.

The farewells were over and the Admiral was climbing the steep steps of the Pullman car again when he suddenly turned and came down. He walked over to me. "Thank you for your help," he said. I replied that I was glad to have been of use. He held out his hand, and I thought he wanted to shake hands with me, but as I extended my hand, he slipped a dollar bill into it. "That's for yourself," he said, and after a brief pause and the suspicion of a smile, he added, "My good man". Then he mounted the steps to the Pullman car. I had accepted the dollar bill as mechanically as he had my five dollars.

The train pulled out and the rest of the delegation marched off smartly; apparently none of them had heard what the Admiral said to me or had realised what was going on between us. I walked thoughtfully out of the station. What was a Second Secretary at the British Embassy supposed to do when he received a tip from a British Admiral? Probably I should have returned it to the finance-and-establishment officer, but I preferred to keep quiet about the whole thing. From the station I went straight to the bar of the Roger Smith Hotel and spent the Admiral's dollar on a dry Martini. In those days you got change for a dollar if you bought a dry Martini; but I don't really know what became of that.

CHAPTER NINE

Life and Letters

---◦◉◦---

ONE of the things that bothered me both at B.I.S. and at the Embassy was the fact that I could take no pride in my own writing, for none of it went out under my own name. I see that in my diary under 23 February 1944 I wrote: "Spent most of the day writing a speech for Lord Halifax to deliver on St David's Day at Scranton, Pa." St David's Day that year kept me very busy; I had to turn myself rapidly into a Welsh expert. On 28 February a mass of material about Wales came in from London and I had to write it up as a press release before the great day (1 March). On 1 March the Director of B.I.S. suddenly decided that an "information paper" on Wales—its history, culture and present situation— should be produced immediately, and I remember dictating it sentence by sentence to the Director's secretary as I composed it. The following week I was much involved in what I described in my diary as the "tedious job" of writing historical notes for a volume of Lord Halifax's speeches. In Washington, after I was transferred from the Information Office of the Embassy to be in charge of educational and cultural affairs, I wrote frequent despatches, all of which went to London under the Ambassador's name. I could not help resenting my anonymity, though this may sound vain and petty. I think that if one is essentially and professionally a writer one resents one's work going out under another's name or appearing as a faceless official pamphlet. But I did take some satisfaction in writing a speech for Field-Marshall Sir John Dill when he received an honorary degree from Princeton University. I did some research on Princeton's history, and I got from my old friend Ged Bentley, who had some time before left Chicago for Princeton, an account of items of current interest at the university and wove this into a witty speech that was full of knowing Princeton references. Later, Sir John wrote to thank me for "making me appear so much wiser than I really am". This was the only time in my B.I.S. and Embassy years that I was ever thanked for ghost writing. Once I wrote a speech on Scotland for a senior member of the Embassy to deliver on St Andrew's Day, but I poured into it so much of my own nostalgia for Scotland that it was turned down as too personal.

There was, however, one occasion where I did appear under my own name, and the result was disastrous. Among our "fifty visitors" we had been advised (I think by one of our film men in B.I.S.) to include Damon Runyon. Normally these invitations, in the form of a standard letter that had been drafted before I came to work in the Embassy, were signed by the Minister, Harold Butler. But he was away when Damon Runyon's invitation was due to go out, and so was Grant Mackenzie, Director of the Information Office whose deputy I was, so that, for the first and only time in the life of the "fifty visitors" scheme, I signed the letter myself. (The letter incidentally, was not in the most elegant English, but my job was to sign the standard letter without any modifications or alterations.) A few days later I was horrified to see that Runyon had viciously mocked the letter of invitation in his syndicated humorous column that was carried by so many American newspapers. As my name appeared at the foot of the letter, he kept returning again and again to the egregious Mr Daiches who had issued him this ludicrous invitation to come over to England so that he could be brain-washed into joining the chorus of Americans who praised gallant little Britain and her great war effort. B.I.S. cabled the column to the Ministry of Information in London, and I received a stern cable from London asking what the hell was going on. Later, I learned from one of the B.I.S. men in London that Runyon was in fact fatally ill (he died the following year) and quite unable to travel, so that an invitation to visit England at war was inappropriate in a particularly ghastly way. We had not been told this in Washington, and the "expert" who recommended his inclusion in our list of visitors was the man really responsible for the whole fiasco, as it was his job to have known. Anyway, I was summoned by Harold Butler to explain the whole thing, and I had a very uncomfortable interview with him. Butler of course realised that, but for the accident of his being away at the time, he would have signed the letter, as he had signed all the others, and would as a result have been publicly mocked by Runyon, so that he could not logically be annoyed with me personally. But he was, understandably, annoyed about the matter in general. Nothing could be done about it, and in a few weeks other important items of Information Office business had driven the Runyon affair out of Butler's mind. But I could never forget it. It was one thing not to get credit for what one had written; it was quite another, and a lot worse, to be publicly mocked for something one had signed but not written. I began to see the point of Ministers taking public responsibility for the actions of civil servants.

In spite of the Runyon affair, I enjoyed taking sole responsibility when both the Director and the Minister were away, which happened at intervals. One especially interesting occasion was on 21 September 1944 when I took Harold Butler's place in visiting the White House to discuss with Steve Early, President Roosevelt's Press Secretary, the timing of an Anglo-American press release on Italy's surrender. Early was very suspicious of me when I arrived. He asked me to produce both my diplomatic card and my B.I.S. identity card, which carried my photograph. But once he was satisfied that I really did represent the Information Office of the British Embassy, we got down briskly to business. This was the only time that I was ever in the White House in the course of my Embassy duties, or indeed in any other capacity. On the other hand, I was frequently at the State Department, particularly after I was put in charge of educational and cultural affairs. I never saw Roosevelt in the flesh, but I once encountered Churchill, when he was staying at the Embassy. It was when I was welcoming a group of American school-teachers who were later to be given a talk on the British educational system, as I have recorded in the previous chapter. Churchill was coming down the imposing Embassy staircase after dinner: red-faced and breathing fumes of brandy, he descended the stairs slightly precariously, holding on to the bannister as he came down. The teachers—all young women—looked up and beheld the legendary figure. Gasps of "ooh!" and "ah!" went up. Churchill looked down at them, and exclaimed: "What a bevy of beautiful maidensh! And sho well behaved! Shuch decorum! Shuch decorum!" (His pronunciation of "s" was not really "sh", but that is the only way in which I can indicate his curiously blurred sibilants.) And he walked past them to the Embassy door, where he entered a waiting car.

Just before I moved from the Information Office to take up my educational and cultural post, I had a brief spell as (among other things) chief information man on economic affairs. The economic plight of Britain as a result of five years total commitment to war was steadily emerging, and the need for a massive American loan to help convert Britain's wartime economy to a viable peace-time economy was becoming increasingly clear —especially after President Truman's sudden and unexpected cutting off of "Lend-Lease" at the end of the war. The Ministry of Information had prepared a mammoth pamphlet, entitled "Statistics of the War Effort", intended largely for distribution in America, which gave all the particulars of Britain's commitment of her resources of both manpower and material to the war. It was an impressive compilation: it was called "Moby Dick" at the Ministry, and an enormous amount of effort went into its production. The aim was to educate American opinion on Britain's plight. Then Lord Keynes was sent over, to discuss prospects of a loan with the Americans. He was then a very sick man, but he did an effective job, not the least part of which was a long briefing of Embassy officials on the precise facts and figures of Britain's economic position. We were told that these figures were strictly confidential and must on no account be revealed, though I could not for the life of me see why not. As my job was to get across to the American press the magnitude of Britain's wartime effort—not easily comprehended in America, a country with sufficiently large resources to have been able to keep a flourishing civilian economy going side by side with wartime activities—I resented what I considered to be needless secrecy about the facts. We had been able to reveal the facts about the past in "Moby Dick", but the facts about the present could only be revealed in the most general terms.

A day or two after attending the briefing by Lord Keynes, with my notebook filled with fascinating facts and figures revealed by Keynes in confidence, I was visited by Tom Twitty, economics correspondent of the *New York Herald-Tribune*. He was planning a full and sympathetic article on Britain's economic position at the end of the war. He had clearly done his homework, and I was impressed in talking with him with his grasp of the whole subject. What he wanted, and what he came to me for, were precise facts and figures that would enable him to present his very pro-British case with full confidence. He said he would not reveal any facts or figures that I gave him off the record, but he had to know them if he was to write with conviction and authority. It was then that I decided, quite deliberately, to violate the confidentiality of the Keynes briefing. I gave Mr Twitty, off the record, all the figures that Keynes had given us. The next morning a splendid article by Twitty appeared on the front page of the *Herald-Tribune*. The Minister summoned me to express his delight. "Now *that's* the sort of article we want to see," he said. "Why don't you get more articles like that into the New York press?" I didn't tell him that the reason the article was so good was that I had given Twitty the full details that I had been told not to reveal. (Twitty, by the way, did not reveal any of the figures I had given him in confidence: but he wrote with obvious knowledge and authority, in a way he could not have done if he had not had the figures.) This was far from the only time that I found security regulations not only silly but positively prejudicial to the British position. I remember pleading in vain to be allowed to reveal the proportion (not the actual numbers) of British troops fighting in South East Asia Command, in order to counter the American impression that only Americans were fighting in the Far East. Security would not let us reveal it, though we learned later that the Japanese had known the figure all along.

It was in the spring of 1945 that I moved from the Information Office of the Embassy to take over educational and cultural affairs from Allardyce Nicoll, who was returning to academic life in the form of the Chair of English at Birmingham after some years as Professor of Drama at Yale. I too was now thinking of returning to academic life, as it was clear by now that the war, in Europe at least, was almost over. I had in fact applied for the Birmingham Chair, and it was only when I asked Nicoll to support me that he told me that he had already been offered the Chair himself. I also applied for the English Chair at Edinburgh, my own university, on Dover Wilson's resignation at about the same time: Sir Herbert Grierson, my old teacher there who had been retired since 1935, had encouraged me to apply when I saw him in Edinburgh in November 1944, when it was already known that Dover Wilson was going to resign soon in order to devote himself entirely to his edition of Shakespeare. I was 32 at the time, and was obviously considered too young (whatever other disadvantages I might also have suffered from), for the Chair went to William Renwick, who was in his late 50s. This was a blow, because I had for long cherished a romantic longing to return to my old university as Professor of English. I was determined to return home and not to settle permanently in America, though many well-meaning friends, both American and British, tried to persuade me that this was a silly and sentimental decision.

Almost every week I received an offer from some American university, which I turned down. I had already resigned my position at Chicago, which had been kept open for me until after the war, on the grounds that I intended to return to Britain. I accepted the cultural and educational job at the Embassy partly because it was interesting in itself and partly as a helpful way of marking time until I could find an appropriate academic position back home. As the months wore on it was borne in upon me that I had well and truly lost my place in the academic queue in Britain and I could only win my way back by developing my reputation as a literary scholar and critic in America. It took me until 1950 to achieve this.

So April 1945 was a fateful month for me. It was fateful for the world, too, for the end of the war in Europe was in sight. Here are some notes from my diary:

April 30. Meeting at 4 p.m. with W. G. Constable to discuss Anglo-American educational exchanges.
May 1. Busy day at the office. News of Hitler's death (if the German announcement is to be believed) came in in the afternoon.
May 2. A meeting this afternoon to discuss exchange of government books and documents between U.K. and U.S.
Berlin finally and totally taken by the Russians today. And the German armies in Italy and western Austria surrendered unconditionally.

On 3 May, after lunching with Neville Gardner of Washington B.I.S. and David Newton of Reuters at the Washington Press Club, I returned to the Embassy to receive a cable from Edinburgh saying that my father had died. This cast a black shadow for me over the victory celebrations that were soon to take place. Those early days in May were very strange. On 16 May I received a letter from my mother telling me that my father had had an operation but was making a good recovery. But it was not until 24 May that I learned the whole story. On that day I received a letter from my mother dated 30 April telling me that my father was gravely ill and there was virtually no hope, and also a letter from my brother-in-law David

Raphael, written the day after my father's death, giving me all the facts. When I returned home from the Embassy on 3 May after having heard of my father's death, my six-year-old son said: "Never mind, Daddy. I'll make you a wooden Daddy."

V-J day, marking the victory over Japan and the war's final ending, was celebrated in a very different atmosphere. I had spent the preceding week on a speaking tour in Kansas, in my capacity as educational and cultural expert at the Embassy. (It was sometimes difficult to distinguish the capacity in which I was invited to speak, particularly at colleges and universities, where I was known for my literary work rather than for my position at the Embassy. But the Embassy took the view that all such invitations were official, and I saw no reason to object to this.) It was on the train on my way back to Washington that I read of the American atomic bombing of Japan, with the details of the first test explosion of the atomic bomb which were now released for the first time. Events now moved very rapidly. On August 14 I recorded in my diary.

All day people awaited the news of Japan's acceptance of the Allies' latest note defining surrender terms. The news tickers at the Embassy poured forth a flood of speculation and noted every movement of every government figure, and the radio had its usual flood of commentators on continuously with nothing to say. Finally at 7 p.m., soon after I arrived home, the official announcement came from the White House that Japan had accepted the Allies' terms and would, therefore, surrender unconditionally. We heard a recording of the speech Attlee made in London, just a few minutes after he actually made it, and then the spate of radio activity to be expected on such an occasion. Reports of frenzied celebrations everywhere kept coming in on the radio. Dr Harris across the way fired off an old German luger he had, and invited us over with some other neighbours for drinks. We stayed there for about an hour. Later, when I was taking Whisky [our Irish terrier] for a walk, I was invited by other neighbours down the road to join one of their parties, so I went in and had a couple of drinks.

We had two days holiday at the Embassy to celebrate, with an official Embassy party on the first of them. I left that party at 7.15 and proceeded to another (alone, for my wife was unable to come as she could not get a baby sitter) given by Caresse Crosby to celebrate the first number of her new periodical *Portfolio*. There were a lot of writers there, and some of us, including Caresse, Thornton Wilder and Harry Thornton Moore, eventually adjourned for drinks and a late dinner at the Trianon. Thornton Wilder and I had both drunk quite a bit, and we got into a furious argument about the relative merits of Virgil and Homer. Wilder was for Virgil, and when I said that Virgil was a sentimental imperialist who couldn't hold a candle to Homer, he crawled under the table, shouting: "Jove, let your thunderbolt fall on *him* not on me. *He* said it. I didn't."

It was in this manner that, on the initial day of peace, we turned our thoughts away from war and back to our first and true love, literature.

CHAPTER TEN

Home

ON 6 October 1944, Harold Butler, the Minister in charge of Information at the Embassy, approved of my going to England on an official visit in order to bring myself up to date on life in wartime Britain. I had been waiting for this for a long time, and I had another month to wait before I actually left, because Butler had suggested that I leave immediately after the Presidential elections (on 7 November), when there would be a lull in the information work. On the night of the 7th I sat up late listening to the election returns as they came in, and went to bed at midnight in the knowledge that Roosevelt was fairly certainly re-elected. By the next morning this was certain, and all of us at the Embassy breathed a great sigh of relief. No other President of the United States at this time was thinkable, either by the British in Washington or by the numerous American officials we were constantly meeting. We never thought of him then as an over-taxed and exhausted man, as we now know he was, and his sudden death the following April was a shocking surprise. By an odd chance, I was one of the first people to learn of Roosevelt's death outside immediate White House and press circles. The news was flashed on the United Press ticker, and I happened to be standing by the ticker, which stood in the corridor of the Information Office, when I saw it tapping out THE PRESIDENT DIED AT (I forgot the exact time it gave) THIS MORNING. It never occurred to me that this referred to Roosevelt. I thought there must have been a reference earlier to the illness of the President of some small South American country and that now they were telling

us that he had died. So I was not unduly alarmed. But just as
I turned to walk down the corridor I heard the ticker's bell
ring—a sign that a really important item was coming—and
went back. The news was repeated (almost as though the ticker
itself had just realised what it had said) in greater detail, beginning: PRESIDENT ROOSEVELT DIED . . . I rushed in to tell the
Minister, who in turn told the Ambassador.

But in November 1944 I had no premonition of what the
following spring would bring—the death of Roosevelt, the death
of Hitler, the death of my father, all in rapid succession. I
was immensely excited at the prospect of getting back to Britain.
I wanted, of course, to see my father and mother, and I wanted
desperately to experience at first hand the quality of daily
living in wartime Britain. I had envied those of my colleagues
who had been sent back home on "refresher courses" and had
interrogated them endlessly on their return to the United States
in order to find out how my extensive second-hand knowledge
of affairs at home correlated with the actual facts. I could never
get enough information. It had been five years since I sailed
on a blacked out ship from Glasgow to New York and, as I
have made sufficiently clear in an earlier chapter, I had often
felt trapped and exiled in America in spite of interesting work,
congenial friends, and the deep satisfactions of family life and
children.

One of my jobs at the Information Office of the Embassy
was to see about transport for officially sponsored travellers
from America to Britain. Where air transport was involved, I
arranged this through Squadron Leader Atherton, the air
attaché, who fixed up passage with R.A.F. Transport Command
from Dorval (the airport for Montreal) to Prestwick. For sea
passage, I had a special telephone line direct to the New York
manager of Cunard. Most of the passengers for whom I was
responsible went on the eastward journey by air and made the
return journey to America, which was arranged by the Ministry
of Information in London, by sea. I now had the immensely
satisfying job of asking Atherton to arrange my official air

passage from Dorval on 10 November. Everything went through
smoothly. My family came to the station with me to see me off
on the train to Montreal, and as the train pulled out my not-
quite-three-year-old daughter shouted, "Bring me back a little
white pussy cat".

On arriving at Prestwick I was allowed to go to Edinburgh
for a few days, to see my parents and also to do some official
work there, before going on to London, where I would be based
on the Ministry of Information. I was of course delighted at the
chance of spending some time in Scotland, for which I had
been desperately nostalgic. I found myself with a devouring
sociological curiosity about the country, of a kind I had never
had before. I was greedy for first-hand knowledge about what
the country and the people were really like under wartime
conditions. Driving in an R.A.F. bus from Prestwick to Glasgow
I looked hungrily at everything—houses and shops and people.
I looked at window curtains, observed the state of cottage
gardens, noticed what was displayed in shop windows, looked
for signs of bomb damage. The day was mild and drizzly, and
an air of damp sadness hung over the countryside. In spite of
having come from safe America into a country that was in the
front line of the war, I had the feeling that I had travelled far
back in time. Everything seemed to belong to an older civilisation. It was all familiar, yet unfamiliar. Things that I had seen
a thousand times in my childhood and youth without paying
any attention now struck me as significant. I noted how many
suburban houses were called "Mayfield". I noticed worn old
advertisements, and a sign that read "Fish Suppers" on a little
cottage shop struck me as being full of social meaning. I was
struck by the solidity of red-sandstone houses and the air of
tidiness and respectability they emanated, and by the vase of
flowers in so many windows. A painted hand pointed to the
bar entrance of a village pub. At Queen Street station there was
still the bustle that had so excited me about railway stations
when I was a child (and which large American stations, with
the station itself carefully insulated from the arrival and depar-

ture platforms, quite lacked). I got into a crowded third-class compartment of the train to Edinburgh, not realising that my voucher entitled me to a first-class seat, and watched the names of familiar stations go by—Linlithgow, Ratho—until the train entered Haymarket tunnel to emerge at last at Waverley Station. I was assiduously helped to get a taxi by an elderly man who evidently assumed, from the R.A.F. sticker on my suitcase, that I was an R.A.F. hero. As the taxi turned into Waverley Bridge and I saw the Scott monument and Princes Street, absolutely unchanged, I felt almost as Scott himself did when, returning from that last hopeless journey abroad, he recognised Gala Water on the road to Abbotsford and sat up with temporarily renewed vigour. As we came up the Bridges to Nicolson Street and South Clerk Street I gazed at the names of shops, so familiar to me from my childhood and my university days, hardly any of them altered. Surgeons Hall, the Old Quad, and then on to Minto Street and Newington Station and my parents' house in Crawfurd Road. I read my father's name on the brass top of the letter-box—the letter-box had come from our family home in Millerfield Place, and was one of my earliest memories—and saw myself as someone who had come back in time as well as space.

I opened the self-locking gate in the way that anybody brought up in Edinburgh knows how to do and walked into the house. I was struck by its Victorian look—the glass on the front door, the size of the rooms, the old-fashioned wallpaper. I found my father and mother upstairs in the drawing-room, huddled over a small electric fire. There was of course a shortage of coal, and no other room in the house was heated. My father, who had been knocked down by a lorry while about to board a tramcar some weeks before, was sitting in an easy chair with his arm in a sling, convalescing. My mother's first words were: "Don't kiss me, I've got a terrible cold". It was just over five years since I had last seen them or Britain.

I spent about a week in Edinburgh, working some of the time in St Andrew's House, where I talked to innumerable officials and discovered some old friends translated to wartime administrative positions. My old history teacher at Watson's was now one of the top men at the Scottish Education Department. Some former fellow students were involved in planning for post-war Scotland, and we talked about housing and agriculture and heavy and light industry with enthusiasm. I had lunch with Dover Wilson, who, since his appointment to the Chair of English at Edinburgh University, had become very pro-Scottish; he urged me to found a secret society for the rejuvenation of Scottish culture. I had tea one gloomy, lowering afternoon with George Kitchin by the window of a restaurant in Princes Street, with the Castle opposite. He pointed to the splendid dark view outside, saying with an ironical sigh, "Mine own romantic town". He told me not to have sentimental dreams of coming back permanently to Edinburgh, since there was no hope of any revival of cultural liveliness in the city, but at the same time suggested that I apply for the Edinburgh Chair of English on Wilson's imminent retirement. I gave a lecture on American attitudes to Britain, organised by the Ministry of Information. I accompanied my mother on shopping expeditions, trying to find out at first-hand exactly what wartime shopping was like. And I bought an ounce of John Cotton's nos. 1 and 2 tobacco at the little tobacconist's shop I had dealt with as a student, and the old lady there said as she handed me my change: "Ye'll have been away?"

About a week later I took the night train to London, where I checked in at the offices of the Ministry of Information in Malet Street (the new administration building of the University of London which had been taken over for the duration). Here there was the same atmosphere of enthusiastic amateurs running a vast information and propaganda machine that I had known at B.I.S., New York. Newspapermen, publishers, film producers, novelists had all come in from their regular professional activities to put their skills at the service of the Ministry. Robin Cruikshank, with a brilliant Fleet Street career behind him, was much involved with the Ministry's

American Division and was devoting the bulk of his energies at this time to the production of "Moby Dick", the enormous white paper giving the facts and figures of the British war effort. George Archibald was worried about the provision of Transatlantic transport for British film people. Herbert Nicholas (now Nuffield Reader in the Comparative Study of Institutions at Oxford) was concerned with the quality and tone of the information we put out for America. Phyllis Bentley was involved with the magazine *Britain*, put out by B.I.S. New York, and complained that it printed too much American material and not enough of the stuff she fed it from London. Hamish Hamilton, the publisher, was at the London end of the "fifty visitors" scheme. I talked with these and many other people in various Malet Street offices, and between such conferences I was taken in a Ministry car on official visits to inspect bomb damage in London.

At this time V.1's (flying bombs or doodlebugs) were still coming over, though in diminishing numbers, but the real threat came from the V.2's (rocket bombs or LRR's), which one heard crashing suddenly without any warning of any kind. I was taken to West Ham, the most badly hit of all London boroughs, where I examined an ARP control room, a Warden's post, a Depot, and of course innumerable ruined buildings. It was a cold drizzly November day, and everything seemed unspeakably melancholy. After looking at the bomb damage I was taken to the Town Hall, where I met the Town Clerk and ARP Controller (one man), before being shown into the Mayor's parlour, a cosy little Victorian room that seemed to bear no relation to what we had just seen. Then the Mayor came in, made some hearty remarks, appended a few religious sentiments, and presented me with a signed copy of *Fifty Years a Borough: The Story of West Ham* before bustling off to a meeting. I was then given lunch in a "British Restaurant" and was able to sample at first hand that wartime institution of which I had written at some length when at B.I.S.

All this was instructive, and I was glad of the opportunity of

gaining the instruction, but what was more important to me
were the opportunities to walk about London, often pub-
crawling and talking to the people in the pubs, and getting the
feel of the city after five years of war. I became highly skilled
at detecting pub doors in the blackout (a more difficult operation than one might imagine on a dark winter night). I learned
something about the relation of GIs to locals, which was useful
for my information work in Washington. And one Saturday
afternoon I walked with my sister and brother-in-law, with
whom I was staying, along Fleet Street and through the Temple
to the Embankment, and landed up having tea at Fuller's in
the Strand. I remember that walk very vividly. In the rapidly
fading light of a late November afternoon the city wore a soft
melancholy air. I felt an almost impersonal sadness, unrelated
to the tragedy of war and destruction and suffering but bound
up somehow with history and the sheer continuity of things.
The way in which the quiet charm of the Temple had survived
heavy bomb damage haunted me in a curious way. I suddenly
felt a sense of warmth towards all who had ever lived there.
I remember too my sense of surprise and pleasure at realising
that after more than five years of war one could still walk into
Fuller's and order tea and toast and cake and be served
reasonably quickly without fuss. It seemed such a quietly civilised
thing to do. Of all my experiences in different parts of England
and Scotland during that visit home in 1944 this Saturday afternoon walk in London stays in my mind as the most *settled*; it
somehow anchored and gave position and proportion to the
other things I saw and did. On another occasion I visited St
Paul's, standing intact amid great devastation, and then went
on to the Guildhall, badly damaged, with the old roof gone
but the main building still standing. I walked through Gresham
Street, Aldermanbury, London Wall and neighbouring streets,
noticing the enormous damage and at the same time being
arrested by some remarkable new views, including St Paul's
from many a new angle. On other walks I noticed bombed
sites that had been made into reservoirs for fire fighters, with

lifebuoys affixed beside them. And twice I heard a V.2 come down fairly nearby, and saw the smoke and dust rising from the new ruins.

The object of my stay in Britain in November and December 1944 was to enable me to familiarise myself with as many aspects as possible of life in Britain under wartime conditions. That was why I was taken to see the bombed East End and given lunch at a British Restaurant. The more I knew at first hand the better I would be (so the argument ran) at my job in the Information Office of the British Embassy in Washington. It was in pursuance of this objective that I was sent out of London for a few days to see something of the R.A.F. at work and of the actual production of planes. I went by train to York, and had time to look over the Minster (with all the stained glass removed) before being driven in an R.A.F. car to a bomber station at Melbourne. Here I inspected the interior of a Halifax bomber, saw parachutes being folded and unfolded in the parachute room (they were made of the most beautiful white silk, a joy to touch), was given a demonstration of the working of a Link trainer, and saw FIDO, the fog dispersal device, before proceeding to the bar of the officers' mess for innumerable drinks. The bar was made from the timbers of a blitzed York pub, and was very cosy indeed. My hosts, R.A.F. officers, did not seem to resent in the least the intrusion of a civilian into their conviviality, but pressed pint after pint of beer on me, followed by a final gin. Then we went in to supper, which was one of the best meals I had during my whole stay in England. After supper we returned to the bar, where drinking and singing went on for hours.

It was a gala night. The boys had been over Essen the previous night, had returned that morning, had a sleep, and had recently got up to celebrate a particularly successful operation. Not a single bomber had been lost. One did not return, but was later reported to have landed safely in France. It was also the twenty-first birthday of an Australian pilot attached to the squadron (10th Bomber Squadron) and that added to the celebratory mood. The squadron, I was told, had been together longer than most, and that perhaps accounted for the particularly intimate spirit that prevailed.

The atmosphere was rather like that of an undergraduate party, except for the note of subdued hysteria that I thought I could detect. Jug after jug of beer was bought and passed round. I had to drink what this pilot and that pressed on me, though it loaded me up considerably, for they were so insistently hospitable that it would have been offensive to refuse. In the course of the conversation, which was general, and on the whole ribald, the Group Captain emerged with a collecting box (for charity) to collect fines from all those—and they were many —who infringed any of the numerous laws regarding what might or might not be said. I gradually gathered that it was a fine-able offence both to brag and to be unduly self-deprecating, and also to mention anything unpleasant such as a disease or an accident. In the course of answering one pilot's questions about Washington, I referred to the tics which produced Rocky Mountain spotted fever, whereupon the shout went up "Half-a-crown! Half-a-crown!" and I had to put my coin in the box. It cost me another shilling when I tried to explain it away.

They brought a piano in about 10 p.m. and then the singing started—all the old bawdy songs I had sung as a student, and some that I had never heard before. For part of the time I relieved one of the pilots at the piano, which brought me still more beer. I was nevertheless sober enough to stand a bit outside myself, as it were, and relish the sight of myself accompanying the singing of an R.A.F. bomber squadron returned from a particularly successful operation over Germany. This was the nearest I got to involvement in that side of the war which was so dear to journalists and broadcasters. It was, partly at least, what I had come home for.

Details of that night stand out vividly in my memory. There was a young officer with a fine tenor voice who sang some good solos, including "Where'er you walk". He would only sing on condition that he could do it as a solo, and I can still hear his voice protesting when some others joined in: "Look here chums, please chaps, I'm only going to sing this if I do it by myself". So they stopped, and he sang alone. It was two in the morning when the party broke up, and I was driven back with three companions to the Station Hotel in York by a very pretty W.A.A.F. driver. The next day I went to Manchester and saw Lancaster bombers being built in the A. V. Roe factory just outside the city.

I had another week in London before going north to Scotland again. I saw Gielgud's *Hamlet*, and a performance of Pinero's *The Magistrate* during which a V.2 came down not far away and the scenery shook violently, but the actors never paused. And at 8.30 on the cold and frosty morning of the 7 December I stepped out of my sleeper at Waverley Station, Edinburgh, for a final few days in Scotland before sailing back to America from Greenock. This time I did not work at St Andrew's House, but was taken around to see aspects of the wartime Scottish scene.

The most memorable of these excursions was a day in Fife, that county where I had spent nearly all my childhood summers and which I knew so well. There was light snow on the ground when the 9.55 a.m. train pulled out of Waverley Station for Kirkcaldy. The countryside was looking its winter best. I crossed the Forth Bridge for the first time since the 31 August 1939, and noticed an aircraft carrier at anchor in the Firth. Once again I devoured the landscape with my eyes, remembering, comparing, re-living, as the train moved along the Fife coast. My destination was the firm of Scottish Plastics Ltd., at Leslie, originally a De La Rue factory for making fountain pens but now making pilot-seats for Spitfires as well as preparing for the conversion of industry to civilian purposes after the war by making, in another section of the factory, a variety of articles from trouser buttons to fountain pens.

I was met at Kirkcaldy by the works manager, Mr Marshall, and driven to Leslie where, after being shown round the factory, I was given lunch at the Station Hotel. There was just Marshall and myself at lunch, in a cosy room with a roaring fire. Double whiskies first, then soup, roast chicken with all the trimmings, stewed fruit with artificial cream, cheese, coffee, and drambuie: if my meal at the R.A.F. officers' mess at Melbourne was the best I had in England, this lunch in Scotland was the best I had in Britain during the whole of my stay. The atmosphere could not have been more different from that of the bomber station. This was an oasis of warmth, comfort and calm in the midst of a cold landscape. Mr Marshall, once he discovered that I knew Fife well and was not a visiting American politician (which for some reason was what he had expected), grew exceedingly cordial and indeed confidential. He told me his life story, and asked me how I would explain a recurring dream he had about his shoe being too big and coming off in the street. Because I was a "doctor of philosophy", he assumed that I knew about such things.

Outside, the scene was like one of those that my wife and I used to pore over nostalgically in the *Scotsman* calendar. As I was driven by an official ministry driver (another beautiful blonde—they all seemed to have gone in for chauffeuring during the war) from Leslie to inspect the modern colliery at Comrie, and saw the Fife countryside whitened by snow so that visibility lingered as the early darkness fell, I had a sense of fulfilment. Here I was, after all those years away: the schoolboy who had spent so many happy days on the Fife coast, exploring rock pools or walking for miles along the shore from one fishing village to another, now back in Fife, being driven in an official car on government affairs.

Three days later I was driven to Glasgow, visiting a new housing estate en route. The next day I was taken over the Colville steel mills. And on the 13 December I found myself standing beside Claud Raines (who had been acting in the film *Caesar and Cleopatra*) in the tender that was taking us to an anonymous ship lying off Greenock. I discovered on boarding that it was the *Ile de France*, run as a troopship by the U.S. Navy, and full of R.C.A.F. men returning to Canada and U.S. servicemen who were classified as R.R.s (home for "rest and

recreation"), "Happy Warriors" (who had done their quota
of bombing missions and could now go home) and "Re-treads"
(mostly older men who had not gone on, and were either being
discharged or posted to positions in the U.S.). Being a diplomat,
I had one of the few bits of fairly decent accommodation left
on the ship, sharing a two-berth cabin with a British brigadier
who was returning to Washington from South East Asia
Command.

It was a weary journey, with the ship, not being in convoy,
swinging far to the south to avoid submarines. I remember
the daily announcement that came over the loud-speaker
system each evening as dusk fell, in an American voice full of
disciplined boredom: "Now hear this. It is 1800 hours, and
blackout regulations are now in force. There will be no smoking
on the open decks and all personnel *on* those decks will go
below." The ship docked at Boston on the 21 December, and
I had the pleasure of getting priority treatment on disembarking
with my diplomatic passport. But the Embassy transport people
had forgotten to get a reservation for me on the night train
from Boston to Washington, so I had to sit up all night in
what must have been the oldest, dirtiest and least comfortable
coach still in service on the U.S. railroads.

Had it all been worth it? Had my fretful longing to be involved in Britain at war been in any way appeased? The answer
to the first question is certainly "yes". My stay in Britain in
November and December 1944 not only gave me a new assurance in talking to American audiences about wartime
Britain but it made me more reconciled to operating from
Washington. I could now say, "When I was in London last
month . . ." I could describe at first-hand what it was like to
hear a V.2 come down. But these were petty egotistical satisfactions. There were deeper ones, too. My visit gave me a
certain emotional reassurance about the nature of my ties to
my native land. But it did not fully appease my sense of guilt
for having spent nearly all of the war in the United States.
It had come too late and lasted too short a time for that.

CHAPTER ELEVEN

Culture and Crisis

EARLY in November 1946 I was back in England to attend the international conference that set up UNESCO. I was not a member of an official delegation, but the Embassy in Washington had persuaded the Foreign Office that I ought to attend the sessions in order to obtain first-hand knowledge of what was going on. I had been very much involved with the Washington end of the preparations for the conference. Indeed, I sometimes think that my one contribution to history was that I may well have been responsible for preventing its indefinite postponement. I wish I could remember the details of the crisis which I was able to resolve, but I see that only the barest outlines are set down in my diary. My wife, in fact, was writing up the diary that week. On Saturday, 13 October she wrote: "David had to arrange to go into the office early to-morrow over a crisis." And on the following Sunday: "David was up at 7.30. No bus for him, but he was able to get a lift to the District Line. Later he phoned from the Embassy to say that the Conference in London was on after all so he is almost certain to be going there at the end of the month".

What happened, as far as I can recollect, was this. On Saturday evening Michael Wright, Head of Chancery, telephoned me at home to say that a cable had just arrived from the Foreign Office saying that the American Ambassador in London had approached our Foreign Secretary with a request that the ECO Conference (that is what it was called at this stage, ECO standing for "Educational and Cultural Organisation") that had long been definitely arranged to take place in London in

November should be indefinitely postponed. What on earth was going on? the Foreign Office wanted to know. The American Ambassador had not given any clear reason for his request, and our people in London were puzzled and annoyed. The Foreign Office wanted us to cable back as soon as possible to give the background to the request and to advise whether or not it should be acceded to. Wright asked me to find out the background as quickly as possible and to meet him at the Embassy early the next morinng to produce a reply to the Foreign Office.

By a happy chance it happened that there was a man at the State Department who was handling ECO Conference affairs who had been an academic at the University of Chicago while I was there and whom I had also seen a great deal of in Washington. He was a good personal friend as well as a colleague. So, after the telephone call from Wright I immediately telephoned this man (I will not give his name, as what he told me was off the record, but he subsequently held quite an important post in UNESCO) and told him of the cable our Embassy had received. Could he please tell me what on earth it was all about? He could and he did. I had the feeling that he was rather glad to let his hair down and let me know that he was aware of the inner goings on in his Department. Archie MacLeish (the poet) was at that time Assistant U.S. Secretary of State, in charge of cultural affairs, and he was soon to be succeeded in this office by Bill Benton, chairman and publisher of the *Encyclopedia Britannica* and formerly Vice-President of the University of Chicago, where I had known him. What I was told was that Benton wanted the conference postponed so that he could lead the U.S. delegation. If it took place at the time originally agreed, MacLeish would have to lead it. This was a question of Benton's personal ambition and had nothing to do with official U.S. policy. What should I advise my Government, I asked my State Department friend, after he had given me this background information in a very racy manner. Turn the request down, he promptly replied. It would throw everything into a state of confusion if this long-planned international conference were to be postponed at the last minute; all sorts of rumours and splits would develop; and it might prove difficult ever to get the conference re-organised. I told all this to the Head of Chancery the next morning, and we concocted a cable to the Foreign Office which ended by advising strongly that the American Ambassador be told that it was too late to postpone the conference. So the conference went on as planned; ECO eventually became UNESCO; and I had played my little part in diplomatic history. Benton was to have the consolation prize of leading the American delegation to the UNESCO Conferences at Paris in 1946 and at Mexico City in 1947.

I was involved in another crisis in connection with this conference. The British Government, as the host, had the responsibility of inviting the governments of the various United Nations countries to send delegations. For some reason they forgot (or perhaps they had never known) that the Republic of the Philippines had become a sovereign and independent state on 4 July 1946 and therefore were entitled to an invitation in their own right and not via the United States. By the time the Foreign Office realised that their omission to invite the Filippino government directly had gravely offended that government the conference was only a week or so away. We received agitated cables at the Washington Embassy suggesting that we help smooth matters over. In the end—and I don't exactly remember by what chain of diplomatic reasoning it was decided that this was the best course—I myself had to draft an official invitation to the Government of the Republic of the Philippines which was sent by our Ambassador on behalf of the British Government. I had never in my life drafted an invitation to one Government from another to attend an international conference, and I did not have the faintest idea what style to employ. After some thought, I invented a rather magniloquent formal style, full of references to both parties in the third person and rolling along in Gibbonian periods. (I employed a similar style many years later in drafting official messages of congratulation from the University of Sussex to other universities in different parts of the world when they were celebrating some anniversary or new beginning.) The Ambassador liked it and signed it, and the Government of the Philippines seem to have liked it equally, for they accepted the invitation with a good grace and all hard feelings were forgotten. The two Filippino delegates actually travelled on the same plane as I did from Montreal to Prestwick, and one of them turned out to have been a student of mine when I was at the University of Chicago!

I flew, as I had the previous year, by R.A.F.T.C. plane from Dorval to Prestwick, making the journey non-stop in thirteen hours exactly and arriving in Prestwick on a soft autumn morning on Sunday, 4 November. After a huge breakfast at the airport (porridge, two kippers, tea and toast with lots of butter and marmalade: I noted this in my diary with wonder, but discovered later that this meal was exceptional and no indication of a substantial improvement of food conditions in Britain since the end of the war) we were flown in an R.A.F. plane to Blackbushe airport near London and then taken into London by R.A.F. bus. I stayed, as before, with my sister and brother-in-law. On Monday morning I reported at the Foreign Office, where I was given a desk at which I was expected to be during working hours for the next month when I was not attending the conference.

I don't think I did any useful work while actually sitting in the Foreign Office, which I found a gloomy and depressing place. But I had many interesting talks with a variety of people outside those sober precincts. I remember a stimulating lunch at the Athenaeum with Frank Cowell of the F.O.'s Cultural Relations Department, a meeting of representatives of universities and of Government departments to discuss the number of foreign students British universities would be able to take, a lively lunch at the English-Speaking Union with that formidable woman Edith Ford, who headed the Committee for the Interchange of Teachers between Britain and the U.S., and other educational and cultural encounters. Of the conference I shall say nothing, as it is all officially documented and I was only an observer. It is the only international conference I have ever attended and I found it immensely interesting. The only thing, however, that I remember actually learning there is that the French for to "second" a motion is "appuyer". I recollect the look of weary scorn that appeared on the faces of some of the French delegates when some of the Latin American delegates (most of whom spoke in French, French and English being the two official languages of the conference) rose to "seconder" a motion.

I went up to Edinburgh for a week-end to see my mother, and it was then that I learned from her those details of my father's death that I record in my earlier autobiographical volume, *Two Worlds*. Then back to London for a few days before leaving on the *Queen Elizabeth* from Southampton.

From my diary:

Just come aboard the *Queen Elizabeth*. And what a luxurious cabin! Large room with private bathroom and two beds (not bunks), I don't know yet who my room-mate is, but the room itself is magnificent—a great contrast to my poky cabin on the *Ile de France* last year. . . . A few minutes after finishing writing the above I got a pleasant surprise on discovering that my cabin-mate was my old friend Macdonald Gordon, Labour Attaché at the Embassy. It's going to make things much pleasanter. . . . The ship is crowded with Canadian army personnel, and there is the usual series of announcements blaring forth from the loud-speaker system all the time. But in spite of all the numerous inconveniences of a troop-ship, it looks as though the voyage is going to be considerably more comfortable than last year's.

It was a pleasant and uneventful voyage, but, as I was later to discover, it did not by any means mark the end of my sea voyages in quasi-wartime conditions of overcrowding and discomfort.

My educational and cultural work at the Embassy kept me in some sort of touch with the academic world, and indeed I had never altogether lost touch with the American (as distinct from the British) academic world even when working at B.I.S., for I used to receive regular invitations to give academic lectures and was able to accept a number of them. By early 1946 it was clear to me that I was not going to be able to get the kind of academic post in Britain that I was anxious to return to. I was reluctant to face this fact, but in the end I had to face both it and its consequences. Unless I wanted to stay indefinitely in my diplomatic position (an option that was open to me), I had to decide what sort of academic position was both possible and desirable. I had long since resigned from my Chicago job, even though the University of Chicago would have kept it open for me until well after the war, and, intellectually exciting as had been my five-and-a-half years there, I did not want to settle there again. I felt that I merited a fairly high ranking academic post. I had now published seven books—three in Britain before I first went to America, and four in the United States of which three were with the University of Chicago Press—the last four of which had won me a considerable reputation. *The Novel and the Modern World*, in particular, had become a standard work, much used and quoted. My book on the translation of the Authorised Version of the Bible could hardly be said to have been popular, but it was a pioneer work of considerable learning in a field which required a variety of linguistic, historical and critical skills to which few of my academic contemporaries could lay claim, and which I owed to the special circumstances of my own background. I had published a fair amount of poetry in *Poetry* (Chicago) and more critical essays than I could remember. I was in continuous demand as an essayist for American periodicals and as a lecturer at American universities. I was thirty-three-years old.

In March 1946 I was invited by Cornell University to go there and deliver a lecture. The idea was that I should lecture on a literary subject (for which the Embassy had no objections to my accepting a fee) but that I should also use the opportunity to speak, perhaps informally to a faculty group, on some aspect of contemporary Britain, as a public relations exercise which would justify my taking time off from my Embassy work. This was, in fact, the formula which had been worked out while I was still at B.I.S. to allow me to accept invitations to speak from universities: I could give a lecture in my own professional area as a literary critic, but I was supposed to use every opportunity to give in addition (and of course without a fee) talks about Britain at war or something of the sort. I did this fairly often in 1944 and 1945. I remember once in 1944 lecturing at Hollins College, Virginia, on some literary subject and in addition giving four other talks to different faculty and student groups on aspects of wartime Britain. This was the only occasion that I ever received an official compliment for my work either at B.I.S. or at the Embassy. The Director of B.I.S., on reading my report of my visit to the college, expressed in writing the wish that everybody working in the Information Division had the ability to make use of such a visit in the way I had done. He considered this ideal activity for an information officer.

My visit to Cornell in 1946 was not my first. I had been invited to speak at the annual dinner of the Book and Bowl, the Cornell literary and social club, some years before when I was still teaching at the University of Chicago. They paid me what was for me at that time the extremely handsome fee of $100. I remember being impressed on that occasion by the beauty of Cornell's physical setting and also by the agreeable atmosphere of cultivated sociability that prevailed during and after the dinner. So when I received this second invitation, I was happy to accept. As it turned out, the informal talk on contemporary Britain proved impossible to arrange, and I contented myself with giving a public lecture on "The Criticism of Fiction". But I discovered, soon after my arrival at Ithaca on the evening of 11 March, that the real purpose of the invitation had been to enable me to meet members of the faculty and the administration so that they could decide whether they wanted to offer me a job. I had a heavy social programme, lunching, dining and having cocktails with various people, including R. C. Bald and Harold Thompson of the English Department, and the Dean and the Vice-President, before a final talk with the President was followed by a concrete proposal from the Dean. It was suggested that they might offer me a full professorship. But the upshot, some weeks later, was a formal offer of an associate professorship. Disappointed, I turned it down, having been led to expect a full professorship. At once Cornell despatched the acting chairman of the English Department to try to talk me into accepting their offer. He came to Washington and spent an evening with me, followed by a lunch together the next day. He pointed out that I had had an assistant professorship at Chicago and that this was a step up; that the situation with respect to some other members of the English Department would make it intolerable if a young man were brought in at a higher rank than they enjoyed; and added that once I was there there would be rapid promotion to a full professorship. In the end, I accepted, on condition that the University would pay the expenses of my family and myself back from Scotland, where we intended to spend the summer.

The decision to accept the Cornell offer meant my definitely giving up hope of an English academic post in the immediate future. It was a real crisis in my life, for my wife and I were both set on returning to Britain after eight-and-a-half years in America. We had originally intended to go there for only three years. But by now some of our closest friends were in America and I was much more part of the American academic scene than of the British. Further, because my last four books, on which my academic claims really rested, had been published in wartime they had not been widely circulated in Britain and as a result my reputation was much higher in America than it was at home. If I wanted (as I did) to return to the academic profession, a job in an American university was inevitable.

But why did I choose Cornell? Though a well-known and beautifully situated university, it was not in the very highest rank of American universities. It had had, and still had, some

world famous figures on its faculty, but it still suffered a bit
in general reputation from Matthew Arnold's quarrel with it
on the grounds of its utilitarian and practical orientation, and
its founder's famous remark that he would found a university
"where any person can find instruction in any study". It had
world-famous colleges of agriculture and engineering and a
school of hotel management that was nationally admired. It
had also had some great names in the humanities, including
Carl Becker in history and Lane Cooper (whom I was to get
to know well when he was in his late eighties) in literature.
Other historic characters as well as Lane Cooper were still
active during my five years at Cornell: Liberty Hyde Bailey,
doyen of American botanists, was born in March 1858 but was
still going strong when he was in his early nineties and I used
to lunch with him on Thursdays as a member of a select
luncheon discussion group. W. F. Willcox the economic statis-
tician was also a member of this group: he celebrated his
ninetieth birthday when I was at Cornell and years later, when
I had left Cornell for Cambridge, visited me in Cambridge en
route to India, where he was determined to see the Taj Mahal
by moonlight, an ambition which he achieved.

But I am jumping ahead. When I accepted the Cornell
offer I did not really know very much about it. But I liked its
situation and its atmosphere, and I liked the people that I met
when I visited it. Some of the members of the English Department I already knew by reputation. I knew Harold Thompson's
work on eighteenth century Scottish literature, a field in which
I myself was much interested, and I knew some of Cecil Bald's
writings on Jacobean drama. I cannot honestly say, however,
that it was the reputation of its English Department that
specially attracted me. In fact, the Cornell English Department
was notoriously disorganised, and rumours of its problems and
internal conflicts were circulating round the American academic world. The situation was so bad, indeed, that it was impossible to appoint a Professor of English as Chairman since
any given appointment would have given offence to others who

thought themselves entitled to it, and the man who came down to Washington to persuade me to accept an associate professorship was the Acting Chairman Tom Bergin, who was Professor of Italian. Bergin's job was to keep the peace and hold the fort until a chairman could be found from among the English professors who would be acceptable to most of his colleagues. (Eventually the job went to Francis Mineka, then an associate professor, who came to Cornell at the same time that I did.) I myself was never a candidate for the chairmanship: an administrative position was the last thing I wanted.

When I ask myself why I went to Cornell and turned down so many offers from other American universities I find it difficult to give a precise answer. It was partly, of course, because the offer came at just the right time. I had just come to realise the impossibility of a job in England for some time and, six months after the end of the war in Japan, I knew that I must soon get out of my wartime job if I did not want to contemplate a radical change in my career. The attractions of the landscape of the Finger Lakes, which reminded me of parts of Scotland, were certainly one factor. I had had enough of the Middle West.

So I accepted an associate professorship at Cornell, to begin the following Autumn. I might add here that I got my full professorship within less than a year of arriving at Cornell. The means by which I achieved this illustrate very clearly the ways of American university administrators. In the spring of 1947 I received from McGill University, Montreal, an offer of a full professorship. McGill wanted somebody trained in Edinburgh, preferably a pupil of H. J. C. Grierson's. But I was just settling down at Cornell and had no desire to go to Canada. (The job eventually went to G. I. Duthie, another Edinburgh graduate.) I mentioned casually to one of my colleagues who dropped into my office the morning I received the letter from McGill that I had received this offer but that I had no intention of accepting it. He got very excited and insisted that I go at once to the Dean and show him the letter. "Why?" I asked. He pointed out to me, somewhat impatiently, that Cornell would surely have to meet McGill's offer and promote me to a full professorship. I replied that this was blackmail, and I couldn't do that, especially as I had no intention of accepting the McGill offer. He laughed and said that everybody did it and that one was *expected* to do it. The University was proud if one of its faculty members received a better offer from another distinguished university. And this was the recognised means of promotion. So, a little uncertainly, I knocked at the door of the Dean's office, and on entering I silently showed him the letter. He read it through carefully, and there was a pause. Then he gave a meditative sigh, look up, and said briskly: "Would a full professorship and another $1,000 be all right?" So I became a full professor just before my thirty-fifth birthday.

After five full and on the whole happy years at Cornell I applied for and obtained a vacant University Lectureship in English at Cambridge. This time it was Cornell's turn to initiate a discussion about promotion. Within minutes of the Dean's receiving my letter of resignation he was in my office assuring me that Cornell would meet Cambridge's offer and asking what my terms were. I explained that Cambridge had not made an offer, but that I had applied for an advertised post at an advertised salary, and had been successful in my application. Furthermore, the Cambridge salary was very much less than I was already getting at Cornell. This was a situation that he simply could not understand. American academic posts, at least those in the senior ranks, are a matter of private bargaining, and one gets the best rank and salary one can by making clear what competitive offers one has received from other universities. The notion that a senior academic could apply for a post with a publicly fixed salary that was lower than what he was getting was incomprehensible to the Dean. He thought that I was holding out for something. The next week he met me in the corridor and said: "Is it an administrative post you want? Would you like to be *Dean*? I'm going to give up the Deanship very soon, and if you would like it—". I hastened to say that I did not want to be Dean. The day before I finally left Cornell the Associate Dean ran into me and said sadly: "We never found out what you were holding out for."

It is easy for the British to sneer at the American system, but there is a great deal to be said for it. It means that an able young man can rise quickly in his profession and does not have to wait for the incumbent of a chair to retire or die before he can have a chair himself. The situation is changing in Britain now, if slowly. But it is not long since there was only one professor in each subject at a British university, with all other members of his department enjoying inferior status with no hope of getting a professorship at that university while the present professor was still there. Some professors would take their appointment as marking the end of their active careers, and they would vegetate quietly while by their very presence blocking promotion for their colleagues, some of whom would very likely be much better than they were and have a much greater reputation. Anyone who knows the British academic scene over the last thirty years can cite instances of this sort of thing.

The American system had its own disadvantages, however. A man who had put down real roots in a particular academic community and was known by the university administration to have done so, could be passed over for promotion on the grounds that he would be unlikely to accept an offer, however attractive, elsewhere. The brilliant teacher and inspirer of students who had published little or nothing so that his work was unknown outside his own university was unlikely to get an outside offer, and so remained at a low rank. I heard of a case where, after an associate professor had bought a house, the Dean was overheard to remark to an intimate that he did not now fear being pressured into promoting the man. There was always the danger that a man's academic worth would be judged by the kind of bid other universities made for him rather than by his actual work for his own university.

My years at the University of Chicago had given me little

insight into the techniques of promotion in American universities, for I had been a special case and did not come under the normal rules. After all, the first person from the University of Chicago whom I had met had been the President himself, whom I had entertained in my rooms at Balliol before I ever thought of crossing the Atlantic; so I had direct access to President Hutchins after I arrived at his university in a way that no one else of my lowly rank had. Once, when I was very broke, I went to Hutchins and asked if I could have some more money. He explained why a salary raise was impossible at that time, but arranged for me to receive $1,000 in two instalments of $500 out of some fund over which he had control. (This was quite different from the $1,000 teaching prize which I mentioned earlier.)

In spite of my preference for a British academic post, I could not suppress a feeling of real excitement when the Cornell appointment was finally settled. I was hungry for the university class-room. I loved teaching, I was confident that I did it well, and the world of students and teachers was my natural environment. But first there was to be a long summer back home in Scotland. One day early in April I wrote my last official letter to the New York manager of Cunard, asking for passage for my family and myself on the *Queen Mary* sailing from New York for Southampton on the following 20 June.

As a locally "hired" member of the Embassy staff, I was not entitled to free passage back to Britain. But I was entitled, with my family, to free transport back to New York, where I had originally been hired by B.I.S. And I did enjoy some very real advantages as a result of my Embassy position. My duty while at the Embassy Information Office to organise transport for important American visitors to Britain gave me an important contact with Cunard. And, while I had eventually to pay for the whole family's transportation across the Atlantic, I did not have to wait in any queue in order to get a passage. What happened was simply that the Cunard manager arranged our passage immediately on receiving my letter, writing me a cordial letter saying that he looked forward eagerly to greeting me himself before I went on board. He presumably took my request for passage as official. Nothing was said about money on either side; but months later I received a handsome bill from the Foreign Office for the cost of the passage, which I paid out of an advance of salary given me by Cornell after I was stuck in Britain six weeks longer than we intended to stay because of a shipping strike in New York.

When we had made our first homeward passage back across the Atlantic, we had had our six-weeks'-old baby son with us. Now we had three children, of whom the youngest, our second daughter, had been born in Washington the previous 17 April, so that she was just over two months old. For the two younger children it was their first visit to Britain, while for the eldest, who was now seven, though it was not actually his first visit, it was the first for all practical purposes, since he had no conscious memory of his months in Scotland in 1939. For my wife, it was her first visit home since then: she had not seen Scotland since that day in September 1939 when the *Cameronia* slid out of Yorkhill Quay, Glasgow, with the painters still at work disguising her colouring. Her father, like mine, had died while we were in America. In spite of my reports, and of frequent letters from her sister, she did not know what sort of Britain to expect.

CHAPTER TWELVE

Renewal

THE first thing I noticed when we docked at Southampton on 26 June 1946 and looked down from the deck at the bustling scene on shore were the words "British Railways" on the side of an engine. This struck me with a great sense of shock. I had rejoiced when the Labour Party had won the 1945 election, and I had supported the nationalisation of the railways, but I had long cherished a romantic feeling for the names of the British railway companies and one of the things I looked forward to was travelling again in those familiarly lettered carriages, S.R., G.W.R. (which I had got to know at Oxford), and, most of all, L.M.S. and L.N.E.R. I even remembered clearly that great change in the early 1920s when so many companies had amalgamated to form this big four. The Midland Railway, the North British, the Caledonian, the Highland line, the Great Northern, which were still friendly names to me, for the older generation had continued to use them long after the amalgamation, while two of them—the North British and the Caledonian—were perpetuated in the names of Edinburgh's two largest hotels. It had not occurred to me that the nationalisation of the railways would have resulted in the wiping out of the names of individual companies and their replacement by a single neutral title lacking all history and romance. Of course, if I had reflected on the matter at all I would have realised that it was inevitable; but I had not, and the sense of loss which I felt that morning as I looked down from the *Queen Mary* was very real.[1]

[1] This is an interesting example of the way in which memory can telescope things. When I wrote this I was sure that the experience occurred in June

Renewal

I was obsessed with a desire to give my small son the opportunity to know and love everything in Britain, and especially in Scotland, that had been significant to me in my own youth. That significance I had only come to realise during my years in America. And British trains were among the things that nostalgia had picked out and lingered on. The sound of British trains was very different from that of American trains, because of the different arrangement of the wheels. In Britain, the two rear pair of wheels of the last carriage and the two front pair of the carriage immediately behind clicked or bumped or rumbled (according to the speed of the train) across the gap between the lengths of rail in a rhythm which from early childhood I had associated with holidays and adventure. The rhythm, once the train had got under way, was reminiscent of the opening bars of Beethoven's Fifth Symphony (ta-ta-ta-TUM, ta-ta-ta-TUM), but it could vary interestingly, sometimes turning to ta-TUM ta-TUM and sometimes TA-ta-ta-TUM. I had explained to Alan, my son, that when we went on an English train he would hear what I called "the true rumbledystum" that could not be heard in America. And sure enough, when our train drew out of Southampton on its way to London and gradually picked up speed, we both heard the true rumbledystum developing, and we sat back in the carriage to enjoy it. I was conscious of being truly happy. At the same time I was fully aware how odd it was that I should be made happy simply by having my small son join me in hearing and appreciating the characteristic noise of a British train.

We spent one night in London before taking the train up to Edinburgh, where a family deputation awaited us. There was my mother, my brother Lionel, recently out of the army, whom I had not seen since 1939, and my wife's sister, now her only surviving close relative. It was an emotion-fraught scene, but all I remember of it is the porter placing the baby in her carry-

1946. But I have since discovered that the change could not have taken place by then, and I was actually recalling our *next* arrival in Southampton in June 1948.

cot on to his truck with the rest of the luggage "to gie the bairn a hurl". The next few days we spent in Edinburgh, and I began my determined re-exploration of the city with Alan, a process which was to be continued on our return to Edinburgh from the north in September. We took tramcars everywhere, and I was immensely gratified when in a short while Alan had learned all the routes and could tell from the number on a tram exactly where it was going. (This introduction of my son to Edinburgh did seem to have had a permanent effect: years later, after he had graduated from Cambridge and embarked on a career as a photographer, he settled in Edinburgh by his own choice, and today he knows the city, which he has often photographed, much more intimately than I, who grew up there, can claim to.)

On 2 July we left Edinburgh to spend just over two months in the little Banffshire seaside town of Cullen, on the Moray Firth. This was not a part of Scotland that I knew well, though I had cycled through it on one of my youth hostel trips in my student days. We had rented a house there through the good offices of my wife's uncle and aunt who had a farm in Cornhill, Banffshire, not very far away. My wife's people came from Banffshire, where she had spent all her childhood holidays: this was her part of the country rather than mine. I had spent most of my summers as a boy on the Fife coast, which I knew intimately and memories of which were a deeply rooted part of my recollections of childhood. But I was glad of the opportunity to get to know another part of Scotland, and indeed the little towns on the coast of the Moray Firth which soon became so familiar to me—Portsoy, Cullen, Portknockie, Findochty— bore many resemblances to the Fife fishing villages I remembered so well, while the differences, in architecture, in local habits, and in the names of the fish one caught from the harbour wall, I found of great interest. But most of all, I felt, I was laying down for my children a host of locally based Scottish holiday memories which could compare with my own memories of Fife. This to me was an absolute need. Because so often the plans of parents in these as in other matters go badly astray, it gives me great happiness, even now, to record that this particular plan worked. I was at Cornell from late 1946 until the summer of 1951, and in 1948 and 1950, as well as each year for some years after we had returned permanently to Britain, we spent our family holiday in Cullen, which became for the children a great storehouse of affectionate memories. They still talk about it with the same romantic nostalgia with which I recall Crail and other villages in Fife.

The clean, washed look of the stone houses in Victoria Street, which sloped down towards the sea, was my first impression on arriving at our new holiday home. I took the two older children for an exploratory ramble while my wife organised things in the house and then, after we had had supper and the children were in bed, my wife and I walked down to the harbour as the sun was setting over the north-west shore of the Moray Firth. That evening remains vividly in my memory. We walked along the quay towards the light at the harbour entrance, which was lit as we approached it. The sea lapped at the harbour wall; the air was soft and mild; we walked hand in hand like a couple of young lovers till we reached the harbour entrance and looked out on the darkening Firth. All the nostalgia for Scotland that had assailed us during our years in America was now appeased. We stayed until it was quite dark, moved and happy. All I record in my diary is "Grand evening". I did not have to write anything down.

The next morning we found the beach. To get there we had to walk several hundred yards along the shore, past a rather messy stretch of sand with lots of seaweed; this was not the real beach, for the sea here came right up to the road at high tide and there was no dry sand. Jennifer, our four-and-a-half-year-old daughter (she is "Jenni" now, but she was always "Jennifer" then) observed that it was not much of a beach to play on, but was delighted with the "big beach" (as she immediately christened it and as we have called it ever since) with its beautiful stretch of sand extending all the way to the cliffs of Portknockie. As we passed the less desirable beach on our way home, she christened it contemptuously "the horrible beach", a somewhat unffair designation which has nevertheless remained over the years as the family name for that section of the shore. We soon grew used to referring to it in a quite ordinary way, with no derogatory meaning intended, as "the horrible beach". So our map of Cullen was soon laid out, with our house, the harbour, the horrible beach and the big beach its significant points. There was also a "horrible bakery", which was a wholly unfair name for a pleasant little bakery in Seafield Street where, one day soon after our arrival, we bought a loaf of bread which happened to have a large hole it in. Jennifer, true to form, at once called it by her favourite adjective, and for years, though we all knew that it was no worse than either of the other two bakeries in the town, it was known among us simply and without prejudice as the horrible bakery.

For me this was a kind of renewal of childhood. I introduced Alan to the mysteries of rock pools and the pleasures of fishing from the harbour wall. At Crail in the 1920s Lionel and I had spent many happy hours on the rocks, exploring the marine life, catching "grannies" and "peoches" (Fife names unknown in Cullen) with our hands, and trying to catch "dairgies" with hook, line and bait. At Cullen we caught "geeks" (young saithe) and "poddles" (larger saithe) and, if we were lucky, large lythe (pollack), and once we took part in the co-operative catching of an enormous conger eel. Occasionally we would go out mackerel fishing with an old fisherman in his boat, baiting the hooks with bits of coloured cloth which were wonderfully attractive to the fish when we ran into a shoal of them. There would be about ten hooks on one line, and in the midst of a shoal one would (with difficulty) haul the line in with a mackerel on each hook: I knew then what Yeats had in mind when he referred to the "mackerel crowded sea". Alan and I would go down to the horrible beach at low tide and dig for lug worms, by far the best bait in fishing from the harbour wall.

Meanwhile my wife was getting used to shopping in a situation which differed very little from wartime. Indeed, in one respect it became worse, because bread rationing was introduced for the first time during our stay in Cullen. We registered at a grocer's in Seafield Street (having got our ration books from the Food Office in Buckie) and from then on it was just a matter of collecting "the rations" each week. But we had one real problem. Elizabeth, the baby, was on an American-devised 'formula' which was based on Carnation milk. We had brought a case of this over with us, but it ran out within a few weeks. I was in charge of this department, and had become used to making the formula under all possible conditions—in ships and trains, in station waiting-rooms, in hotels, in other people's kitchens. I followed the doctor's prescription for increasing the proportion of milk as Elizabeth grew older, and she throve on the progressively richer mixture that I gave her. And then the Carnation milk ran out.

When I mentioned the problem to my wife, she pointed out that she had been saving points—canned goods were rationed on the points system—for precisely this eventuality and she would see what she could do. An hour later she came from her shopping with the news that Mr Ingram, the grocer, had laughed ironically when she asked for Carnation milk or an equivalent brand. Points or no points, he had said, no canned milk was to be had. He had added that it might be possible for us to get from the Food Office in Buckie (a larger town further along the coast) a card entitling us to National Dried Milk, but he wasn't sure even of that, because, after all, we were transients.

"National Dried Milk!" I exclaimed. "But how can I work dried milk into a formula that calls for thick, wet milk? The two are not commensurable." I thought of asking a British doctor for a substitute formula, but then I decided to stick as far as possible to the one prescribed by our American doctor. So I determined to make a real effort to locate some canned milk.

Later that day, I found in Seatown, the part of Cullen where the fishermen lived, a shop in which I was able, after much pleading, to get two cans of a variety of milk that had exactly the same milk and cream content as a can of Carnation milk. (Elizabeth was consuming a can a day by this time.) The following day, I took a bus to Buckie, bent upon ransacking every corner of the town for canned milk. I was lucky. The second shop I entered, which happened to be the Co-operative, had a shelf-ful of canned milk, and, to my astonishment and joy, the man behind the counter was willing to let me take away as much as I could carry, if I had points for it. The milk had been laid in, he told me, for trawler crews, who used a great deal of canned milk on their fishing trips, but they had gone off without this lot and he thought they must be all stocked up now for the season. He was, in fact, glad to get rid of the stuff. Aside from the fishermen, none of the local people would touch it. I produced my ration books, and then staggered out of the shop with twenty-four large cans of milk.

As soon as I reached home, I went into the kitchen and dumped the twenty-four cans triumphantly on the table. "There"! I said to my wife. "And look what big cans they are. There's at least a month's food for Elizabeth there."

No sooner had I uttered these words than I was struck by the disturbing thought that if the cans were larger than Carnation milk and the formula called for so much water and so much "Dextrimaltose" to one can of Carnation milk, I would have some trouble getting the right proportions. I called for an empty Carnation milk can, studied the legend on its outside, and compared it with that on one of the cans of milk I had just bought. This milk, I discovered, came from Ireland. And not only did the contents of each can amount to something like a third more than was contained in each Carnation can but the proportion of cream was greater. Further, one was measured in fluid ounces and the other in parts of a pint. I did not see how I was going to convert so much of a pint of canned milk of one cream content into so many fluid ounces of canned milk of another cream content. An additional complication was that British pints are not the same as American pints; they are determined by the size of the imperial gallon, which is roughly a fifth more than the American gallon. Clearly, I had a formidable proportion sum on my hands. I can no longer remember the exact quantities involved, but I remember all too distinctly my feeling of despair when I sat down with paper and pencil to work out Elizabeth's formula in terms of the Irish milk.

In 1929 I had won my Scottish Higher Leaving Certificate, and my subjects included mathematics. I had not really calculated since then. Desperately I tried to dredge up any mathematical bits that might help me. I think in the end I must have gone right back to those first principles that Archimedes or Ptolemy or some of the other ancient founders of mathematics so painfully worked out. I constructed a series of equations stating the relationship between weight and volume of milk, and the relationship between different volumes of milk of the same cream content and between the same volumes of milk with different cream contents. After several hours, I evolved an equation designed to yield the amount of Irish milk that was the equivalent of one can of Carnation milk. "Let x equal the amount of Irish milk desired . . ." And finally, using this equation, I mixed up the formula and stilled Elizabeth's hungry cries with what turned out to be a wholly satisfactory bottle.

Three days later, I came to the end of the last of the two or three cans of "Dextrimaltose" we had brought from Washington. I anticipated no trouble in getting *that* at Findlay's, the local chemists, and sure enough, when I went there and told Mr Findlay what I wanted he produced a tin immediately and I bore it happily away. But when I looked at it at home I saw that it was labelled not "Dextrimaltose" but "Maltidextrose". Nothing that I could discover from reading the information on either the new can or the old gave any indication as to whether these were identical substances or not. I went back to Mr Findlay and asked his opinion, but all he could tell me—apart from a genial assurance that it was the same sort of thing and perfectly all right—was that there was a No. 1, to be given under ordinary circumstances, and a No. 2, to be given if the baby found No. 1 too laxative. Perhaps it was the other way round. Anyway, this sent me home again to examine the old can—"Dextrimaltose"—and I found that it was No. 2. So back I went to Mr Findlay and exchanged the No. 1 he had originally sold me for a No. 2, assuming that the same principle held in both brands. When I got home this time, I read the legends on the two cans once again and realised that the numbers were exactly reversed—the American brand specified No. 2 for the conditions that required No. 1 of the English brand, and vice versa. By now, I was thoroughly fed up. I didn't mention the discrepancy to my wife, and mixed the formula with the No. 2 can of "Maltidextrose". Elizabeth continued to thrive.

The Irish milk gave out a week or so before we left Cullen, and though I returned to the Co-op in Buckie, there was no more to be had. (Presumably the trawlermen had come back for the rest of the milk after all.) By this time, however, my friends and relatives in Edinburgh had been advised of the position, and had rallied round, collecting odd tins of Carnation milk from their grocers. They sent these to us, and I reverted to the original formula.

I had better complete the odd saga of Elizabeth's formula, although it means jumping a bit ahead. We were due to sail back to America, where I was to take up my new post at Cornell, early in September, but a strike upset the sailing of ships and the sailing for which we had reservations (it was the first westbound passage of the *America*) was cancelled. The result was that unexpectedly we spent September and most of October in Edinburgh. My mother had sold the large family house soon after my father's death in 1945 and had moved to a flat, where, to her sorrow, she was unable to put us up, so we stayed in a boarding house in Newington Road while awaiting news of our passage. The other rooms in the boarding house were for some time taken up by delegates to a conference of Baptist ministers, who kept the children awake at night singing hymns. But the real problem was where to make the formula. Our rooms were small and cluttered, and while the woman who ran the place offered to fix the baby's milk herself in the kitchen, she scorned the idea (which we had learned to respect religiously in America) of sterilising the bottles. This, naturally, outraged me, and later my wife and I hit upon the expedient of my going up the road where an uncle and aunt of mine lived and making the formula in their large and commodious kitchen. (My mother's flat was in Heriot Row, on the other side of Edinburgh, so going there to make it was impracticable.) Every morning, then, I could have been seen walking up Newington Road carrying a zipper bag full of the materials necessary for making the formula. So far, so good. But by about 10 September 1946, the Carnation milk collected with such care by my friends and relatives was exhausted. Once again I searched the shops for more of it or of similar brands, but without success.

There was nothing for it this time but to use National Dried Milk. My wife went to the Edinburgh Food Office and explained the situation. She was told that, as a visitor, she was not really entitled to National Dried Milk, but under the circumstances she would be given a ration card enabling her to get it. She came back with the card and a huge silver-coloured tin of the stuff, purchased at the Food Office for a purely nominal sum. I seized the tin and perused the instructions. They told me how to reconstitute the milk with water, and what strength to feed infants of different ages, but gave me no data on the basis of which I could work out the amount of reconstituted milk that was equivalent to one can of Carnation milk. Further, amounts were given only for each individual feeding, instead of for a twenty-four hours' supply (the American formula had involved making a twenty-four hours' batch at one go). I could, of course, have abandoned the original formula completely and simply followed the instructions on the dried-milk can. But these seemed to me to be based on an entirely different principle, and I was not sure how Elizabeth would react to the sudden change. There must be some way of solving the conversion problem, I thought. Eventually, I found it. I discovered a way of relating both the dried milk and the canned milk to fresh cow's milk of average cream content; after that, it was a matter of writing out and solving a number of algebraic equations. (At school, I remembered, I had been reproved for solving arithmetical problems by algebra.)

The story became even more complicated later on, when my wife lost her milk-ration card and we could therefore no longer get National Dried Milk. We solved that problem eventually by buying "Humanized Trufood" at Boot's the Chemist—an expensive and cowardly way out, I could not help feeling, but Elizabeth throve on it as she had thrived on everything else we had tried. In these days when we are all so conscious of starving children in many parts of the world it seems ridiculous to have got so hot and bothered about quantities and proportions. I suppose that my concern indicated some degree of Americanisation on this point. All our three children had been born in America, and we had accepted implicitly the American doctrines about proportions and sterilisation, as we had the American term 'formula' for the contents of a baby's bottle. We thought the British were backward in these matters. In 1939, when we were home with our single young baby and he was lying in his pram outside my parents' house in Edinburgh, our old family doctor, who had so often attended me as a child, came to visit my father and stopped on his way in to have a word with the infant. He stuck his forefinger into the infant's mouth, and the infant sucked vigorously on it. The doctor laughed. "That's the way to tell if they're hungry," he said cheerfully as he passed through the front door. But my wife and I were horrified.

I don't think, however, that we were Americanised to any significant extent (for better or worse) in any other respect. We fell quickly into the rhythms of Scottish life, even though it involved my wife's getting used to what was still virtually a wartime economy. But there was always my wife's uncle's farm, Nethermills, at Cornhill, about twenty miles away, where we could buy as many eggs as we wanted and where we used frequently to get a present of a chicken. After nearly a quarter of a century the children still remember the glories of a "Nethermills tea". It was always a Scottish farmhouse high-tea of legendary lavishness and variety, rationing or no rationing. My wife had many relations who farmed in that corner of Banffshire, and during our first weeks in Cullen we made the rounds, sampling the lavish country hospitality. We had no car, and went by bus, sometimes walking a considerable part of the way. Sometimes a cousin of my wife's would meet us at the nearest bus stop with his car.

There was one cousin who was not a farmer, but a rubber planter who was home from Malaya on extended leave after spending a large part of the war in a Japanese prisoner-of-war camp. The rubber company who employed him gave him masses of back pay on his liberation, and as a result he spent money freely on his return to Scotland. He lived in Portsoy, only a few miles from Cullen, and he had acquired a car. In spite of stringent petrol rationing, he seemed always to have plenty of petrol. He took us many a "ron" (as the Banffshire people pronounce "run") in his car, including a memorable one when he and I engaged to have a drink in every Gordon Arms between Cornhill and Tomintoul. We returned to the farm at Cornhill rather merry (if I had known anything about driving then, which I did not, I would have been terrified). My wife's uncle-by-marriage was with no great difficulty induced to accompany us on the last leg of our trip, to the Cornhill Gordon Arms, a simple rustic hostelry. There he consumed a fair amount of whisky, though he was still far behind William and myself. He was a wonderful old man, with a pure Banffshire accent and a vocabulary which included Scots words I had seen in my reading of early Scottish literature but had never before heard. Until this evening he had always been slightly distant with me: after all, I was a "professor", and he regarded me with a certain amount of awe, though he was just over twice my age. But that evening broke down all barriers between us. As we came back from the village pub to the farm, he said: "David, I never really kennt ye afore: I thocht ye were een o' they releegious chappies that didna tak a dram!" The country people tended to confound ministers and professors. An even older uncle-by-marriage of my wife's said to me when I first met him: "Ye look aafy young to be a meenister." Then, after a pause, he added: "Och, but it's no a meenister ye are, it's a professor."

CHAPTER THIRTEEN

Cornell

B ECAUSE of the shipping strike to which I have referred,
we spent nearly two more months in Scotland in 1946
than we had intended. We were supposed to return to
the United States early in September, but in fact we finally
left at the end of October. We left Cullen on 10 September,
and spent the rest of our period of waiting in Edinburgh, where
day after day I retraced with my young son Alan my own youthful footsteps. We went out along the Forth to Port Seton, walked
over the Pentlands, had tea in Balerno, visited Roslin Castle.
It was on our return from a visit to Roslin on the mild evening
of 23 October that I found awaiting me a telegram from the
Foreign Office announcing that they were keeping reservations
for us on the *Aquitania* sailing for New York on the 27th. What
had happened was that, as the prospects of our getting to
Cornell before the end of the term in which I was to begin my
new job there kept fading, I had begun to think of other ways
of getting passage to America. (This was still before regular
Transatlantic sailings had been restored, and we were dependent
on our reservation on the *United States*, whose sailing kept being
postponed.) Of course I was enjoying these bonus weeks in
Edinburgh, but I knew they were expecting me at Cornell, and
I was also a bit worried about Alan's schooling, though I gave
him daily lessons myself. So I wrote to Michael Wright, who
was now back at the Foreign Office, asking official help in
getting a passage, on the grounds that my taking up the Cornell
position was in the interests of Anglo-American relations. By
a happy chance, the Foreign Office had chartered the *Aquitania*

175

(on what I think was to be its last run before it went to the breaker's yard) to take a large British delegation to the United Nations, as well as other official British visitors, and Wright was able to arrange for us to get passage on this voyage. We sailed on 27 October and arrived in New York on 2 November.

Once at Cornell, where the "semester" had long been under way, I plunged *in medias res* with a fine abandon. I had three courses, one on Shakespeare, one on "great English writers" (Chaucer, Shakespeare, Milton, Pope and others), and a graduate seminar on eighteenth-century literature. The first two, which were undergraduate courses, were taken by substitutes in my absence; the third awaited my arrival before starting. "I had my first class today: talked about Chaucer, the Wife of Bath's Prologue, with negligible preparation," I recorded in my diary for 7 November, but I have a more vivid memory of taking over the Shakespeare lectures from my substitute the following day. He had been doing *Julius Caesar* and had almost finished. He asked me to allow him to finish the play before I took over, pointing out that he needed only another ten minutes or so. I had no objection, so I sat in the front seat while he summarised the action of the last scene of the play, quoted a few lines, and then read extracts from various critics. I thought it a very dull performance and was determined to enliven the proceedings as soon as I got started. He took about fifteen minutes, then he briefly introduced me and left the rostrum. A certain romantic aura surrounded the new young British professor who had been delayed in Scotland by a shipping strike, and everybody wanted to know what I would turn out to be like. I strode to the platform and without a note or a copy of the play before me started to talk about the meaning of the end of the play. I was excited; my ideas came welling up with great force and clarity; I spoke with vigour and eloquence. I saw the class sit up. Years later, when I lectured at the Sorbonne, one of the professors there said to me afterwards: "Vous avez electrifié nos étudiants". I think the same could have been said of the reaction of those Cornell students. I was showing off,

I suppose; but I did so much want to make a real impression on my audience. There was no doubt of my success. That lecture virtually established my reputation among Cornell students and from that day forward I was regarded as an eloquent, persuasive, lively, original, somewhat wayward lecturer whose lectures should not be missed.

At none of the other universities where I have taught have I enjoyed quite such a reputation. Eventually, everybody wanted to sign up for the classes that I taught. When, the following term, I taught a course in modern English fiction an enormous crowd of hundreds of students turned up at the opening lecture and I had to devise a test in order to eliminate those who had not got the background knowledge to enable them to follow the course properly. The same thing happened the following year with my course on twentieth-century English poetry. The eighteenth-century seminar I turned into a study of eighteenth-century Scottish poetry, concentrating on Allan Ramsay, Fergusson and Burns, and these were little enough known in Cornell to ensure that the seminar was small and manageable. I enjoyed this seminar, but in a quite different way from the lectures. A quite different kind of teaching skill was involved. The lectures involved both presenting material logically and vividly and thinking aloud on the critical meaning of what was presented in as persuasive and stimulating a manner as possible. They were public performances. The seminars were intimate discussions, and the graduate students who participated in them had done some serious reading in the subject before they came.

It was easy to deceive oneself about the effectiveness of the lectures. A rapt and enthusiastic audience did not necessarily mean an understanding audience, and I remember some terrible moments of disillusion when I read in examination answers what some members of my heart-warming audience really got out of the lectures I imagined they had been following so perceptively. I used to pride myself on holding the attention of students when I lectured; it took me some time to discover that holding the attention is not quite the same thing as ensuring an intelligent understanding of an argument that has been put forward. The trouble was that many members of my audience had had no proper previous training in the subject. The American system allows students with negligible background in a given subject to attend a university course in it, even though advanced courses are often restricted to those who have the 'pre-requisites'. I remember once opening a course of lectures on modern poetry before an audience of over three hundred people with a sketch of the history of the language of English poetry which was a deliberate *tour de force*, designed to discourage those among my audience who had not the background to follow the references, allusions, quotations, parodies and ironies. I was trying to reduce the numbers of the class by frightening off those who could not follow. One very bright student, who had been in other of my courses, came to my office afterwards and reproved me for giving a brilliant lecture that was beyond the conprehension of many in the audience. "You mustn't do that," he said reproachfully. "You talk so interestingly that they think they understand you, but they really don't. They don't know enough." I took this as a kind of compliment, for even while I was trying to get rid of the students who were not equipped to follow what I was saying (at the beginning of a semester there was always a week's grace for students to change courses), I wanted to impress and excite them by what I was saying. Vanity on my part, I suppose, but I think a good teacher is always something of an exhibitionist.

There were divisions in the Cornell English Department, but they were more personal and less ideological than they had been in Chicago. I took no part in these divisions, being equally friendly with all parties. In any case, the circle of friends that we soon made was not confined to the English Department. We soon had linguists, historians, philosophers, musicologists, anthropologists, political scientists and physicists among the friends with whom we regularly exchanged dinner invitations. And then there was the "Vicious Circle", a select discussion-group of people representative of different academic disciplines, which had just been formed when I came to Cornell and which eventually grew in importance to be a major force in policy making in the university. Henry Guerlac, the historian of science, Max Black, the philosopher, Mario Einaudi, the political scientist, Mike Abrams, the literary scholar and critic, were some of the members. We met monthly in each others' houses, one member reading a paper before general discussion. I am not much of a "joiner", and have become less so as I have grown older. Most societies I have joined have turned out at some stage to be a chore or a bore. But the Vicious Circle never was. I look back on its meetings with unadulterated pleasure, and today when I re-visit Cornell—nearly twenty years after I left it—I am invited back into the group as though I had never left.

In spite of dissensions within the English Department and elsewhere, there was a university spirit at Cornell of a kind I had not found at Chicago. The battles of Chicago had all been intellectual, and I had not been aware of any university spirit overriding individual differences. Hutchins had set his face against university football and the whole "Rah! Rah!" attitude that went with it. In many obvious respects this was a good thing: nothing in American universities is more tedious than this kind of flag-waving loyalty associated with semi-drunken alumni at football games (never football "matches" in America) and ridiculous cheer-leaders organising carefully prepared spontaneous demonstrations. There was something of this at Cornell, but something else as well. That something else derived, I think, from the University's physical location, in a small town (which it dominated), on a hill overlooking a lake. The town of Ithaca, New York, was in large measure dependent on the University, and the University permeated the town in all sorts of ways. This fact brought a kind of unity to an institution which was in fact made up of very diverse elements. Partly a privately endowed university and partly a land grant college, Cornell University had some sections of it financed by the State

of New York and others privately financed. The College of Arts
and Sciences, with which I was most concerned, was in the
private sector, though it was able to get money from the public
sector by such means as charging the College of Agriculture
(financed by the State) for those of its students whom it taught
"Freshman English".

Some of the Cornell students at the lower end of the ability
scale were pretty poor—poorer than any I could remember at
Chicago. I myself never taught "Freshman English", that
course in reading and writing that Americans for some reason
seemed to prefer to teach at the first-year university level
rather than at the secondary school level: I did not in any
case consider this proper university work at all. I taught "upper-
classmen" (i.e., students in the third and fourth years of their
four-year B.A. programme), occasionally sophomores (second-
year students), and graduates. Though there was a considerable
tail in many of the undergraduate classes I taught, the students
at the top were sometimes very bright indeed, sometimes (like
Harold Bloom, who is now a professor at Yale) brilliant. There
were two distinguishable streams of undergraduates at Cornell:
the bright city boys and, less often, girls, from New York City
(often Jewish), self-confident, competitive, constantly on the
look-out for intellectual stimulation, and those from up-state
country areas, who had had a much less good secondary education and were besides intellectually slower. There was also an
element of moneyed snobbery and fraternity exclusiveness with
which I came into little contact but which I know existed at
Cornell though to a lesser degree than at some other of the
so-called Ivy League universities.

There was something about Cornell that commanded a kind
of loyalty, even from distinguished scholars dedicated entirely
to their subject, that I had not found at Chicago. Mike Abrams,
one of the most devoted literary scholars and critics I know,
whose work on romanticism has been internationally acclaimed,
was (and is) a passionate Cornell patriot for whom the University, both in its physical actuality and in its spirit and

atmosphere, is something that commands a deep affection. It was with him that I went to my first American Football game (no member of the Faculty at the University of Chicago ever showed any interest in football) and first heard the crowd sing, with genuine emotion, the Cornell song, "Far above Cayuga's waters". For the only time in my life I became infected with that variety of group spirit that prevails at American university football games. And walking back among the crowd from the stadium on a cold, darkening late-autumn afternoon after a Cornell football victory over Princeton, with bright lights in the windows and signs of celebration and festivity meeting us at every turn, I felt myself part of an American community in a way I very rarely did throughout all my years in the United States. There was something seductive about Cornell, and I felt it strongly, even though I never wavered in my determination to return to Britain as soon as the proper kind of academic position turned up there.

In spite of my total lack of any ambition to become involved in administration, I did become involved in a slight degree when I became chairman of the newly created Division of Literature in 1948. The idea of the Division of Literature was to provide courses that cut across the different national literatures (many of which were represented by wholly independent departments). Such courses had in fact been given for some time, and had been arranged by a committee. But now it was proposed to build up an administrative structure that would organise and administer many more such courses, and I was asked to be in charge of it. I was given a small budget, to provide a part-time secretary for myself and pay the salary of a new professor who would range over the different European literatures. This was supposed to be only a beginning, but in fact, during my time at least, the Division of Literature remained a pretty small affair, with no build-up of new appointments. This was largely because some literature departments were annoyed at what they considered to be the threat to their autonomy and there was as a result much politicking against the Division of Literature. At one point the Dean was anxious to turn the Division into a Department of Comparative Literature with myself as chairman. (Old Emeritus Professor Lane Cooper was indignant at the title, arguing with impeccable logic that there was no such literature as comparative literature, that "comparative" referred to a way of studying literature, and that the title should be Department of the Comparative Study of Literature.) But this plan, too, proved abortive, and I was left as chairman of a somewhat anomalous organisation.

The disquiet aroused by the Division of Literature among some of the literature departments was partly the result of a fear that the Division would play a role analagous to that played by the powerful and still growing Division of Modern Languages, which had taken over language teaching from the departments of French, German, and so on, in order to concentrate it in the hands of linguists who had no necessary interest in literature at all. The fight between linguists and men of letters was a bitter one at Cornell, and it reflected a debate that was going on all over the country.

At the time that I was appointed Chairman of the Division of Literature, Morris Bishop, Professor of French Literature, had been for some time anxious to bring his friend Vladimir Nabokov to Cornell. As a writer and critic who was a master of Russian, German, French and English and who had written in all those languages, Nabokov seemed an appropriate person to give courses in various aspects of modern European literature of the kind that the Division of Literature was trying to encourage. He had been teaching at Wellesley College for seven years, so he had academic experience. Morris Bishop talked to the Dean and the Dean talked to me and the three of us talked to each other, and the upshot was that Nabokov became the first full-time member of the Division of Literature at Cornell. I remember my first meeting with him at a party at the Bishops, where he was introduced with some trepidation to his future colleagues. A jovial, rather bucolic looking figure he was, standing with his back to the fireplace, correcting mispronunciations of his name by those members of the faculty who insisted on stressing the first instead of the second syllable.

Nabokov was not appointed specifically to teach Russian. He was regarded rather as a writer and critic knowledgeable in European literature who could teach such courses as "The European Novel". Of course, he taught some Russian literature as well, but if there had been any expectation that he would teach Russian language courses this was quickly dissipated when it became clear that Nabokov had no opinion at all of the Cornell modern linguists and despised equally their methods, their point of view, and their intellectual equipment. For him language was an extremely subtle and sensitive instrument whose potentialities could best be tested and illuminated by its use in imaginative literature; he viewed with extreme distaste an approach to the Russian or any other language based on an analysis of phonemes and morphemes.

There was no Russian Department at Cornell and Nabokov was not (as has sometimes been said) in charge of such a department. Every other professor of literature belonged to a department—English, Romance Languages, Classics, etc.—but Nabokov alone had no department. He was, as they said, "carried" on my budget, the Division of Literature budget, as an Associate Professor in that Division. The position was anomalous, and I think he felt it. But of course he was an anomalous figure altogether in the academic world. His brilliant and idio-syncratic lectures on the European novel, reflecting a highly original and very unacademic approach, puzzled some students and enchanted others. The examinations he set produced despair among many of those who had to sit them; they used to come to me and complain that they could not understand what Nabokov was after. His critical views were both un-American and un-English. I remember him and his wife Vera proclaiming authoritatively at an academic dinner party that Jane Austen was a grotesquely over-rated novelist and that there were dozens of deservedly forgotten minor novelists in nineteenth century France who wrote her kind of novel better than she did.[1] No one could say that he was not stimulating.

In one respect, however, Nabokov was very conventionally academic: he had the traditional academic lack of ability to cope with the practical affairs of daily life. He never drove a car; his wife did that. He never even carried his books to the lecture room: his wife did that too. She also marked his students' papers, a menial task which he found distasteful. Yet, though she managed his practical affairs, she was by far the more aristocratic figure of the two, with the kind of beautiful fine-boned face that age cannot mar.

The Nabokovs never seemed to me to be really settled at Cornell. So far as I can remember, during their years they always lived in quarters rented from some temporarily absent professor. They never had enough money. Almost weekly Nabokov would come into my office and explain that he could not make ends meet and ask if I could arrange for him to have a raise in salary. Each year, as I made out the budget for the Division of Literature, I put in a substantial raise for Nabokov, and almost every time the higher administrative authorities— who, I am afraid, regarded Nabokov as an optional luxury in the university—turned it down. No aspect of Nabokov's later emergence as a best-selling novelist gave me greater personal satisfaction than the realisation that he would now be free of those besetting financial worries. Years later, when I was at Cambridge, I met him at a party given for him by the Provost of King's soon after the publication of *Lolita*, and noted how happily he filled his true non-academic role of literary celebrity and how the still beautiful Vera radiated a kind of pride and assurance that I had never quite seen in her at Cornell. Not that she ever lacked pride in her husband (while possessing a shrewd critical mind of her own): after carrying his books to

[1] Yet he included *Mansfield Park* in his course on "Masterpieces of European Fiction". The other works were *Dead Souls, Bleak House, Madame Bovary* and *The Death of Ivan Ilyich* in the first term and *Dr Jekyll and Mr Hyde, The Overcoat* (Gogol), *The Metamorphosis* (Katka), *Swann's Way* and *Ulysses* in the second.

his lectures at Cornell she would put them on his desk and then sit appreciatively among the students to listen to him. But now he was something else, something better, I am sure they both felt, than a university professor.

Nabokov's relationship with America has always seemed to me ambiguous. He positively despised most American academics, especially those professors of literature with an inadequate knowledge of the language of the European literature they taught. He always seemed to me—for all his relish of America, for all his huge appreciation of the oddities, absurdities, glories, contradictions and peculiarities of American life and culture—a deeply European person. And deeply Russian too, though a Russian who looked back on his lost country in the light of a strong and extremely personal kind of imagination.

Nabokov was a curiously robust aesthete, a combination which bewildered many of his Cornell colleagues. Literature for him was a way of exploiting and dominating language, not of expressing attitudes. I remember him best at Cornell as a genial but always surprising talker at dinner parties, and especially one occasion at our house when, on tasting a rice dish prepared by my wife, he turned in a business-like way to Vera and asked her why *she* could not prepare rice like that. There was no sharpness in the inquiry, just a good-natured desire to push another practical problem of life on to his wife's shoulders. They were a splendidly loyal couple, and I like to think of them now free both from the financial stringencies and the academic responsibilities of the Cornell phase of their life, free denizens at last of the international Western world of letters.

A friend who read this account of Nabokov shortly after I first wrote it, returned it with this note: "The only words of Nabokov that you recall are 'Why can't you cook rice like this?' Surely during your years as a colleague of Nabokov's at Cornell you heard him speak more immortal words than these?" But the plain fact is that I didn't. We very rarely discussed literature. I heard him talk enthusiastically about butterflies more than once. When he heard that my wife and I came from Scotland he remarked in a tone of bored aloofness that Scotland had very few varieties of butterflies and was virtually a desert, lepidopterally speaking.

During my five years at Cornell I was continually meeting writers and men of letters of all kinds, not only when they visited the University but when I lectured at other universities and at writers' conferences, which I did often, or when I participated in Columbia Broadcasting System's classic Sunday morning cultural programme, "Invitation to Learning". One of the most interesting of these many encounters was my first meeting with Robert Frost, which started a friendship that lasted till his death though we were only to meet two more times. It was in July 1949, and I was giving some lectures at the Breadloaf School of English at Breadloaf College, Vermont. At my first lecture (on modern poetry) I discovered that Robert Frost, who lived nearby, was in the audience. I had just published a long review of the new collected edition of his poems, and it pleased him enormously, especially my discussion of the influence on him of the Latin poets and my comparison of him to the elder Cato. So he had decided to come and hear me, and liked what he heard. The result was that I spent two days with him at his cottage in Ripton, Vermont, during which he was in a consistent good humour (not a common thing with him) and talked about himself with remarkable freedom. Indeed, I discovered later in talking with Larry Thompson, Frost's official biographer, who must have spent altogether hundreds more hours with Frost than I did, that Frost confided to me some details of his life that he had not revealed to him. I wrote down what Frost said as soon as I was free to do so, and these are the notes I made (excluding certain libellous statements about some living people):

He had started on a poem that morning, but had given it up. "If I can't make it go at once, I don't go back to it again." It began: "Going into the woods to work" (or perhaps it was

"Going once into the woods to work") and its point was to be that you find things (e.g., rare wild flowers) in the woods when you go there to do a job (e.g., cut wood) that you don't find when you go specifically to look for them.

He never farmed in England, as some people have written, though he had a garden. He was a close friend of Edward Thomas. Thomas was killed in the attack on Vimy Ridge: the ridge had been taken and he heard the cheers of the men just before he was hit by a stray piece of shrapnel. He was filling his pipe at the time, sitting down.

Thomas saw the war as a release, and joined up for active service at the front in spite of the efforts of influential friends to get him a safe job. His father knew Lloyd George and had arranged for Thomas to get a safe job, but Thomas wasn't having any. At the beginning of the war he got a job listening in pubs to find out how ordinary people were taking the war: it was for some periodical (which?). When he returned from being interviewed for it he was met by his wife and Frost. His wife was jubilantly excited that he had got the job, but Thomas himself was sullen and unhappy about it, and refused to share her joy. Her enthusiasm angered him, and they quarrelled, going home separately. Frost took Mrs Thomas home (they cycled).

Ezra Pound "made over" Yeats. "I saw it happen." He shut Yeats up for two years, and then he emerged a quite different kind of man and poet—hard, even bitter, anti-romantic.

Pound wrote to Lascelles Abercrombie after Abercrombie had written an article in defence of Milton. The letter said (roughly): "Human stupidity carried beyond a certain degree becomes an affront to the public. I have assumed the public's quarrel. Please choose your weapons." Abercrombie was much taken aback. Frost pointed out that the man challenged had the right to choose weapons, and someone (Frost?) suggested that they should fight with unsold copies of each other's books. Amy Lowell, who disliked Pound, went to him after he had

written this letter and scared him by saying that since Abercrombie could choose his weapons, he would not choose swords
since he knew that Pound had described himself as a master
of fence: he would choose pistols. Pound: "Surely he wouldn't
do anything so dastardly!" Lowell: "He certainly will. You'd
better get ready to leave the country." Pound paled, and
packed his bag. And that is the story of how and why Pound
left England. (This, said Frost, was told him by Amy Lowell.
Did she invent it?)

Pound used to bring out his tin bath and have a bath in the
middle of the floor in the presence of visitors. He was always
very abusive. He got fed up with England and went to France;
got fed up with France and went to Italy. He now alleges
(Frost continued ironically) that he was fed up with Italy and
hated Mussolini.

Pound wrote to Norman Cousins in the middle 1920s asking
for a regular job on the *Saturday Review of Literature*. In his letter
he said that the English poets were no good, and went through
them all, giving an abusive description of each. Cousins was
scared to take him on, though Frost said he should. Pound
said he would take $1,200 a year.

Going to visit A.E. in Dublin, Frost entered the room, where
Yeats was talking with A.E. He heard Yeats say: "A.E., we must
absolve the stars".

Frost said that all great poetry had the accent of conversation, and quoted *Macbeth* "(Ye secret, black and midnight
hags," etc.) and *Lycidas* ("Begin then, sisters of the sacred well"
up to and including "Hence with denial vain and coy excuse").

Of Yeats's phrase "perne in a gyre" he remarked that since
one didn't know what these strange words meant, the phrase
was a defect in the poem (*Sailing to Byzantium*).

A man called me a bastard Vermonter the other day (said
Frost), and I called him a Vermont bastard. He isn't interested
in whether his country is New Hampshire or Vermont. The
whole regional business amuses him. He was born in San
Francisco. The family doctor said he would die in childhood

so they didn't bother to send him to school for his first twelve years. As a result, he learned to read very late. He used to go down town with his father and eat his sandwich lunch with him at saloon counters. His mother was born in Leith. He described his solid training in Latin grammar at high school, by a woman teacher. He was taught Virgil for the grammar merely: "Nobody told us it was great literature." He used to resent this, and refused to subscribe to a memorial to his teacher, but now thinks it may have been a good thing: he could later come to the works and, reading them in the original, discover their greatness for himself.

He is interested in Scotland, especially in the Orkneys. He was much impressed with Eric Linklater's *Men of Ness* and was very interested in my account of Linklater, about whom he knew nothing save that he had written this one book. I promised to send him some of Linklater's other novels.

F. S. Flint (said Frost) translated Sorel's *Reflections on Violence* for T. E. Hulme. Flint was really the pioneer, the man who brought over *vers libre* from France: he was very well up in the French poets. In a sense, Flint and not Hulme was the father of the whole business (i.e., the Imagist movement and subsequent developments in modern poetry). Frost suggested that I write an article claiming the whole glory for Flint—it would be fun. Flint (added Frost) was a mild old man now.

Frost talked with Eliot (I think, on his recent visit to the U.S.). Some people there were asking Eliot's views on various poets, and he was throwing them out one after another. Asked about Burns, Eliot said that Burns was not a poet at all. "But would you say he was a song writer?" pursued the questioner. "I think we may allow him that modest claim," replied Eliot.

Frost asked me to send him one of my books ("one that isn't too expensive"). "I don't thank people for writing about me, but I want to say that I was pleased by your review." He said how pleased he was by my reference to the influence on him of Latin poetry, which, he added, too few people had recognised. He pointed to a shelf of Latin authors (mostly Leob editions) among his books. This was his last gesture as I left the cottage.

Some eight months later I had a very different kind of experience with a very different kind of poet. Dylan Thomas arrived at Ithaca by plane from New York at 3.5 p.m. on Tuesday, 14 March. A colleague and I met him at the airport (I was to take the chair at his poetry-reading that evening). At first we could find no sign of him. After it became clear that all passengers who wanted to disembark had disembarked, my colleague and I, who had been assured by telegram that Dylan had been put on the plane at Newark airport, entered the plane to see if he had mistaken his point of departure. We found him slumped in his seat, more than half-asleep. He had been taking sleeping pills as a cure for air-sickness.

We took him back to our flat, where he called for cold beer to revive him. I thought some fresh air would do him good, and he agreed to go for a walk round the picturesque Cornell campus, which was looking especially beautiful with snow on the ground and a cloudless blue sky. We walked over the suspension bridge to my office, and we talked about village life and the pros and cons of being a village worthy. Just as we entered Goldwin Smith Hall, where my office was, he complained of feeling sick again, and before I could stop him he had taken a number of pills from his pocket, crammed them into his mouth, and washed them down with water from the drinking fountain that stood near the entrance. He explained that he had been prescribed sleeping pills by a doctor in New York, for he was unable to sleep in the centrally heated hotel bedroom, yet if he opened the window to relieve the stuffiness the noise of the traffic was equally effective in keeping him awake. So he got a large bottle of sleeping pills, which he was now using to cure sickness caused by flying with a hangover. I was horrified at this dangerous practice, and hurried him home. By this time he was almost asleep again. We put him into Alan's bed, and he was still asleep when guests arrived for the dinner party we were giving so that people could meet him. We went right through dinner without Dylan. His poetry-reading was due at eight o'clock, and I knew that one of the biggest halls in the university would be packed to hear him. The guests left to go to the reading, and Dylan was still in bed. I went in, found him more or less awake, got him up, fed him black coffee. I finally got him to the hall about five minutes late, to find, as I had anticipated, the hall absolutely full. Dylan looked terrible. He sat by me as I introduced him. I was sure that he was in no fit state to give a poetry-reading, and thought that the best I could do would be to explain and apologise. So I explained how, coming from austerity Britain, he had been subjected to the competitive entertaining of New York writers and critics, and was naturally suffering from exhaustion. I put it as tactfully as I could, but I was really warning the audience that the speaker of the evening was in no fit state to give a poetry-reading. Then Dylan got up, moved sluggishly to the lectern, and began to talk. At once he became a totally changed person. His voice vibrated, his eye cleared, he dominated his audience. He proceeded to give a brilliant series of readings from his own and others' poems, a truly remarkable performance which held the audience entranced. He certainly made a fool out of me. "I'm just an old ham," he said afterwards when I asked him how he was able to do it. "I respond to an audience."

We had invited quite a large number of people to meet Dylan over drinks after the poetry-reading, as only a few could be accommodated at dinner. Dylan remained in excellent form throughout this party; he was agreeable and gentle, with none of the wild pranks for which he was so notorious. When my wife said how sorry she was that she had been unable to get to his reading, since she had to prepare for the evening party, he at once offered to read, especially for her, whatever poem she chose. She chose *Poem in October*, and he read it superbly, better than I have ever heard since on recordings; then he wrote an affectionate inscription to us both in our copy of

A Third World

The World I Breathe. (A London bookseller recently offered me £75 for this copy, but it is not for sale.)

He was catching a train to the west that night, and at about eleven o'clock one of my colleagues drove him to the station at Syracuse, N.Y., where one could get on to the New York Central line. He professed to have forgotten the name of the station where he was to get off and the name of the man who was to meet him. Once on the train, he sat down on his bunk and terrified himself with thoughts of moving out into the night, forever westward, further and further away from anything familiar. "I think I shall die in Utah", he said, just before the train pulled out. He had told me earlier that he thought he was going to die fairly soon and that he could not help feeling that his poetic career was almost over.

The next day I wrote to John Brinnin in New York urging that someone be sent with Dylan on his travels to keep an eye on him, since he had formed the habit of using sleeping-pills as a cure for a hangover or air-sickness or both. I thought that the combination of alcohol and sleeping pills might eventually prove fatal. When I heard of the circumstances of his death in November 1953, I thought I knew the real cause.

CHAPTER FOURTEEN

Educating the Children

—◦◉◦—

ALL our three children were born in the United States,
Alan and Jennifer (Jenni) in Chicago and Elizabeth
(Liz) in Washington. We had their births duly registered
at the appropriate British consulate, so that they have British
citizenship. But British citizenship is a pretty notional idea
when you are a three-year-old playing with your contemporaries on the sidewalks of Chicago or a six-year-old in an
American grade school. In his fourth year Alan made friends
with two miniature gangsters some three years older than he
was, whom he greatly admired and with whom he used to
play outside. They were known as Toody and Dubsy (I am
not sure about the spelling, as I never saw the names spelt)
and I suspect that now they are either millionaires or languish-
ing in some penal institution. Alan admired them enormously,
which made it all the easier for them to extract from him his
more expensive toys. I remember in particular one splendid
cowboy pistol and belt. The pistol was a large, silver-coloured
repeating affair, well and ingeniously made. It had been, I
think, a birthday present, and we had spent a lot on it. Once
Alan began sporting it on his person, it took Toody and Dubsy
one short afternoon to relieve him of it permanently, by a
system of "exchange" in terms of which Alan received a piece
of worthless rubbish. We were very angry when we discovered
what had happened, but Alan was quite content. Some years
later, when we were in Washington and he was six, an older
boy whom he liked and trusted relieved him of his bus
money when the two of them went on an expedition into

the centre of Bethesda, and he had to walk several miles home.

Such things happen, of course, in all countries. But for us they seemed to emphasise the Americanness of the environment in which our children moved. Alan started school in Washington, and because we thought that at any time we would be returning permanently to Britain, we sent him to a fairly small private school so that he would be more or less kept up to the standard that would be expected of someone of his age when he crossed the Atlantic. When, instead of going home, we went to Ithaca, N.Y., both Alan and later Jenni went to the local public school there. (I need hardly add that in America "public school" means something more literal and very different from its British meaning.) We did not live up on Cayuga Heights, the prosperous residential part of Ithaca, but down below in Cayuga Street, in the bottom half of quite a pleasant old frame house. The local school served the rather tough neighbourhood which was contiguous with ours. Alan would report with complete nonchalance on expeditions made by friends of his to steal candy and (of all things) pens from a nearby store. Colleagues of mine urged me not to take a high British moralising line about schoolchildren stealing: they all did it, they said; it was part of the fun of being young. There was another side to it. Alan used to talk about a special friend of his, a boy of his own age, so my wife asked him to ask the boy to come to tea and sent a note for the boy to give to his mother to make the invitation official. She prepared a fine spread. But the boy never turned up. It occurred to my wife that the boy might have been a Negro, for there were quite a lot of Negroes at the school, and that there might have been some social shyness involved. So she asked Alan if his friend was coloured. He replied: "I didn't notice. Do you want me to go back and look?" So much for any theory of innate colour prejudice. From earliest childhood Alan had no social or racial prejudices of any kind, and I like to think that this characteristic, which has remained with him, is a legacy of his American years.

It was not the social problems that worried me, but the educational. The American system was fine for pre-school children (what Giuseppe Borgese used to call "the play stage of education") and for research-minded graduates, but less good in the in-between stages. Neither in primary nor in secondary education, it seemed to me, did the American child in the public schools, to which over ninety per cent of all American children went, learn enough. He emerged insufficiently literate and insufficiently equipped with basic linguistic and mathematical skills. The existence of "freshman English" courses at virtually all American universities was certainly testimony to the plain fact that most American secondary schools did not teach their pupils to read and write properly. Some of the teachers our children had in America were talented and some were dedicated. But neither in the first Ithaca school to which we sent Alan nor in the Cayuga Heights School to which both Alan and Jenni went after we moved up the hill in July 1949 did I feel that the children were being *taught* much. Their intellectual curiosity was not satisfied and their learning potential virtually ignored. I have always believed that an intelligent child properly taught will enjoy learning, and will be able to acquire a range of basic skills (among which I was especially interested in the linguistic) that will provide an invaluable foundation for later education. (When I say that he will "enjoy learning", I do not mean that all stages of all a child's learning processes are "fun" and that there is a royal road to the acquisition of knowledge, skills and understanding. I mean that a child, even where hard work and sustained concentration are involved, will, under the proper conditions, enjoy the awareness of acquiring knowledge and understanding, of satisfying intellectual curiosity and learning new skills.)

The result was that I felt responsible for making good by my own teaching any of the school's deficiencies. But there was another factor in my decision to do some teaching myself. Readers of my earlier autobiographical book, *Two Worlds*, may recall that my father, great scholar though he was, was not a

A Third World

gifted teacher and did not succeed in passing on to my brother
and myself his great range of languages and other knowledge.
I had very largely to teach myself, because of my ambition
and my pride, certain branches of knowledge which I could
have absorbed from him if there had been the right kind of
regular communication between us. He was so anxious to put
behind him his continental background and to put down roots
in Scotland that it sometimes seemed as though he was directing
his children away from areas of knowledge that were too intimately connected with certain aspects of his own past (though
I don't for a moment believe that he was ever conscious of
doing this). I wanted desperately to avoid this mistake. I
wanted my children to have everything that I could give them
and I particularly wanted them to appreciate the cultural
riches of their combined Jewish-Scottish ancestry. I have mentioned in an earlier chapter how anxious I was that Alan
should get to know and love Scotland, and how happily that
particular ambition was fulfilled. But I also wanted him to
know Hebrew, and to learn it from *me*, not from some American-
Jewish Sunday-school teacher with whose approach to almost
everything I would probably be in total disagreement. And I
wanted him to acquire a good reading knowledge of Latin and
Greek, which I knew he would not be likely to get in an
American school. I could see, too, that he was musical, as
happily all our children are, and I wanted him to learn to
play a musical instrument well.

The upshot was that I behaved rather like James Mill with
his son John Stuart, though I did not start Alan quite so young.
He must have been about seven when I started him on Latin.
By this time he had also started learning the violin. And I had
already started to teach him Hebrew. Every morning I got up
before 7.00, and from 7.00 until 7.45 Alan and I would have
lessons. We would have Latin and Hebrew on alternate days,
twenty to twenty-five minutes to each, and the remainder of
the period would be devoted to practising music together. I
would take out my violin and would play his exercises with

196

him, or else accompany him on the piano. By the time the family sat down to breakfast at eight o'clock he had done more serious work than he was likely to do for the rest of the day. And I felt that I had done my morning's duty as a parent. Some three years later I added Greek to the curriculum, having first been most scrupulous to ask Alan whether he wanted to add this further language. Surprisingly, he had said "yes".

The experiment ended when we decided, after much debate and heart-searching, to send Alan home to Scotland to go to school. We felt that he was getting bored and discontented at Cayuga Heights School. He didn't seem to be learning anything there, and, I confess, I was getting a bit exhausted with my own teaching (I had now added practising the piano daily with Jennifer). Both my wife and I disapproved of boarding schools, but we thought that this was a special case. In the end, we sent him to Gordonstoun, in close proximity to my wife's farming relatives in Banffshire. (He went first to the preparatory school at Aberlour.) He already knew this part of the country, as we had spent holidays in Banffshire in 1946, 1948 and 1950, in the autumn of which last year he entered Aberlour. I met Kurt Hahn, Gordonstoun's founder, and though I thought that some of his ideas were a bit half-baked, I liked the atmosphere of his school, which had none of the offensive features of the normal English Public School. I also got the impression that the special problems Alan would face, with his particular background and his American experience, would be sympathetically handled, and that there would be no attempt to fit him into an official school mould. I wrote at length to the headmaster at Aberlour about what I had done with Alan up to that point, and hoped that those foundations would be built on. As it turned out, they were not, for a variety of reasons.

Three months after we had left Alan alone in Scotland—it had been a terrible experience, returning to America without him, leaving him in Edinburgh with my mother—I received news about my Cambridge appointment, so that we were all back permanently in Britain the following summer. The previous summer, 1950, I had fulfilled a long-standing promise to Alan by cycling with him right round Scotland. We used to chant Latin declensions and conjugations or declaim Latin sentences as we sped along. I thought that now he was going to a "real" school I need not worry any more. The foundations had been laid. But there was a long gap before Alan started Latin at school and by that time he had forgotten most of what I had taught him. And he never learned Greek at school at all. His Hebrew also, unexercised, grew dim. It turned out that Alan's real interests were history and the visual arts, especially the latter. When eventually he found his own *métier* as a photographer he began to work in an area in which those strenuous morning lessons were of no use to him.

For some years I reproached myself with having demanded too much of a small boy. Though I regularly helped Jenni with her piano playing I decided not to give her formal morning lessons as I had done with Alan. With Liz there was no problem, because we were already settled in Cambridge by the time she was of school age. Ironically, Jenni was the one whose mind turned out to be most like mine; she did Latin and Greek at school and enjoyed both, and if I had worked with her as I had with Alan she really would have built on the foundation. As it was, I confined myself to reading Virgil with her when she was preparing for her "A" level Latin examination.

My self-reproaches about Alan were suddenly removed one evening a few years ago shortly after his marriage. I was talking with him and his wife about the problem of educating children and reminiscing about those early morning sessions. I explained that I had been so anxious to hand on everything I could, because of my disappointment that my father had not done that for me, that I had rather overdone it. To my surprise, Alan denied this. He said the only mistake I made was to stop. I should have gone on, he said; I was giving him much more than he ever got at school. He reproached me, in fact, not for doing a James Mill on him but for having given up doing so too soon. "But didn't you find it a strain?" I asked. "Even if I did," he replied, "you should have gone on. I may have been too young to appreciate what I was getting, but I would have appreciated it later." He really sounded aggrieved that I had not pushed on with those lessons in Latin, Greek and Hebrew.

It is of course a mistake to try and fulfil your own earlier ambitions through your children. Yet I do believe that parents should try to hand on everything they know, by all means at their command. Formal teaching is only one means, and that perhaps not the most important. A home atmosphere in which books, conversation (even argument) and music play a large part was something that both I and my children grew up in, and I think it did us all good. There has also always been in our family an atmosphere of verbal humour—puns, crazy rhymes, parodies, private words—which sometimes puzzles and bewilders outsiders. I had this as a child, too. Someone once said to me in America, after I had improvised a tri-lingual punning limerick: "I've discovered the clue to you; you're a word man". I think there is some truth in this. But it's nice, if you're a word-man, to have a word-wife and three word-children. For one thing, it prevented any suspicion of a generation gap—the more so since the youngest is the wordiest.

CHAPTER FIFTEEN

Entry and Departure

WE were back in Scotland in the summer of 1948, spending two months in Cullen. Once again we had trouble in getting return passage to the United States. We had applied very early for passage on the *Washington*, the United States Line ship on which we had made the eastward journey in early June, and months later found that we had not been given passage because (or so we were told) the company had got their file turned upsidedown in some redecorating spree and as a result had given passage to those who applied last and none to those who applied first. By the time we discovered this, it was too late to get passage in any other of the few ships that were making the westward Transatlantic run at a convenient time. Finally, in desperation, I sought the assistance of a friend and former colleague who was then cultural attaché at the United States Embassy in London, pointing out that when I had held a similar position at the British Embassy in Washington I had got scarce passage on British ships for American academics who wanted to go to Britain to do research immediately after the war. The result was that we were given passage on the *Marine Falcon*, a former "liberty ship" (one of those constructed at great speed during the war) which was being used largely to transport students.

The *Marine Falcon* was not constructed as a passenger ship, and our voyage in it was not exactly comfortable. We ran into a hurricane half-way across the Atlantic, and the ship went miles out of her course, to the south, in an attempt to dodge it which almost succeeded. Our steward told us that the ship,

being welded and not riveted, might split in two at any moment. But we finally passed Ambrose Light at 2.10 p.m. on Sunday, 18 September, eleven days after leaving Southampton. There followed the most unhappy entry into the United States that I have ever experienced.

The ship's arrival was evidently unexpected, for when we docked at 4.45 p.m. there were no customary officials preparing themselves to process the passengers before letting them disembark. They did not arrive until about 5.30. They quickly processed all the American citizens and let them go off the ship. The rest of us—immigrants, visitors, returning resident aliens, and miscellaneous non-Americans—were told to wait in line outside the main dining-room. We meekly ranged ourselves in a line, and waited. Our last meal had been an early lunch at 11 a.m. so we were all feeling a bit peckish. There were mothers with whimpering babies in their arms, and everybody was impatient and even unhappy. At 6.30 the doors of the dining-room were flung open and we got a glimpse of the immigration officials, their uniforms comfortably unbuttoned, finishing what smelt like a hearty dinner. Several children cried as the smells came out of the door, and a teen-age girl left the line to see if she could get the chef to make some sandwiches for the queuing non-Americans. (She returned twenty minutes later with a large pile of corned beef sandwiches which she distributed with a fine impartiality up and down the line.)

Having allowed us to watch them finish their dinner, the immigration officials then slowly prepared themselves to interrogate us. I had been through many interrogations by American immigration officials, and had always found them courteous and efficient, but this lot seemed to be offensively official. Four different officers interrogated each passenger, and there was an atmosphere about the interrogation that I had never met before and that I did not like. We finally got off the ship about eight o'clock, with ourselves and our three children utterly famished.

The customs officer was pleasant enough, though he did make us open every single thing, and we would have got through that stage with reasonable speed if Alan's violin had not got mislaid. We found it, after half an hour's searching, under the letter "Y". By 9.00 p.m. we were through, and, exhausted but thankful, got into a taxi. I was wondering whether the hotel had kept the reservation I had made by cable from the ship: I knew they did not guarantee them after eight o'clock. And it was not easy to find rooms in a New York hotel late in the evening in September 1948.

The taxi had just started when I realised that I did not have my briefcase with me. As this contained all our passports, re-entry permits, and other documents testifying to our official existence, discovery of its loss shook me considerably. I asked the driver to stop, and he agreed to wait while I dashed back to the customs shed to try and find it. The shed was emptying now, and I dashed wildly up and down, accosting every uni-formed person I encountered and asking if he had seen a black briefcase. Nobody had. I had almost given up when, gyrating for the fourth time round the shed, I passed the letter "Y" and saw, all by itself in the now empty section, my briefacse standing on the floor. I had put it down there and left it when retrieving Alan's violin.

I seized the briefcase and ran madly out of the shed, conscious of the taxi's metre ticking up and of the increasing improba-bility of the hotel's having kept our reservation. I was almost out of the shed when I ran plump into the arms of a huge policeman who said, with heavily ironic politeness: "Ju-u-u-u-st a minute, Bud."

"Look," I said, "I've been back here to find my briefcase, which I left by mistake. I have my wife and kids waiting in a taxi outside, and it's late and we're all tired and in a hurry." And I made as though to dash forward again.

"So you're in a hurry, eh?" he asked, stopping me again.

"Yes I am," I said, "and please don't interfere with—"

"Just come this way, will you?" he said, seizing my arm with a vicious grip. "I'd just like to see what's in that precious brief-case of yours."

"I'll show you," I said, opening it and scrabbling for the papers inside. "It's my passport and—"

"I'll take a look," he said, taking the briefcase from me. We were in some kind of room or alcove off the customs shed by now; but I was too angry and upset to notice where exactly he had taken me.

He searched my person thoroughly and then looked carefully through the passport. I was still (though no longer accurately) described in it as "Second Secretary at His Majesty's Embassy in Washington," and the diplomatic visa, though no longer valid, was clearly stamped in an obvious page. The policeman then took out a letter which was folded inside my passport: it was from the Dean of Humanities at Cornell offering me my Cornell professorship. He read it, replaced it in the passport which he replaced in the briefcase, and handed me the briefcase back. He was embarrassed.

"I'm sorry, sir," he said, "but that running out of the customs shed, pretending you'd forgotten something, is an old dodge. Sure sign of a smuggler." He had his arm over my shoulder now and was escorting me back to the taxi. "Dope, you know," he added confidentially. "That's what I was looking for. And let me give you some advice, sir. Never run out of a customs shed, and specially not with a briefcase." He patted me on the back, and left me.

"You found the briefcase?" asked my wife, as I got into the taxi.

"Yes," I replied weakly, and held it up. The taxi driver started off.

"The driver was saying," said my wife, "that there's no hope of our still getting our reservations at this time of night."

"Nope," said the driver. "But don't you worry. I'll get a room for you. I'll fix you up nicely."

"But—but—What kind of a room? Where? A decent place?" I asked.

The taxi-driver turned his neck to look coldly at me. "When I recommend a place it's a decent place," he said. "Nobody can call me indecent."

"All right," I said. "But I want you to go to the hotel first, just to see if they mightn't have kept our reservations."

"Waste of time," said the driver.

"Still, I'd rather you did," I insisted.

"Okay, okay," said the driver. "But it'll be no use. Just cost you more money." And he sullenly drove us to the hotel.

As he pulled up outside the hotel entrance, I told him that I would dash in and inquire at the desk whether they had held our reservations, and if they had not he could take us to the place he recommended. So I got out of the taxi and ran into the hotel lobby. The first thing I saw was a queue of some fifty people at the registration desk, lining up for rooms. My heart sank. But I was damned if I was going to trust that taxi driver—I don't exactly know why, but I was soured on all officials and that included taxi drivers—so I ran out again and said, mustering an enthusiastic tone, "Yes, it's all right; they've kept our reservation".

It seemed to me that the taxi driver snarled at this, and he looked down with a sneer as I disembarked my wife and children and unloaded our copious baggage; he even objected to the handsome tip I gave him, pointing out that he had waited while I looked for my briefcase and thus missed several other fares. I hastily gave him another fifty cents, for I felt that if I left him too disgruntled he would somehow manage to prevent us from entering the hotel and whisk us off to his own recommended rooms, which loomed in my imagination as not only physically shabby and morally shady but also sinister in a purely Poe-like sense. The hotel porter came out at last and took care of our baggage, and I ushered my weary family into the hotel lobby.

The queue at the desk was longer than ever, but I went up to the front and, hoping desperately against hope, accosted the room clerk.

"I don't want to jump the queue," I said, "but I do want to know if you've kept our reservations, because if you haven't we've got to start looking for another place at once. We've just got off the ship, and the children are dropping with hunger and fatigue."

In my anxiety I forgot even to give my name, but the clerk tumbled to it with a magical efficiency.

"Ah," he said brightly. "Mr Daiches and family off the *Marine Falcon*. We heard that it docked late this afternoon. Of course we have your rooms, sir." He collected some keys and pinged the bell beside him, shouting "Front!" "And I'll send a maid up to help your wife get the children settled down," he added.

The next ten minutes were like the moments in the English Christmas pantomime after the good fairy appears and suddenly changes the heroine's lot from tremulous anxiety to comfortable splendour. Somehow milk and sandwiches appeared in the children's room, and somehow they were fed, washed, and in bed. I believe the promised maid did appear and help with these matters, but all I really remember is sitting exhausted in a chair and seeing things take care of themselves. I was roused by my wife suggesting that I take a shower and change and then go down with her to the bar for a drink.

The bar, Manhattan cocktail architecture at its most discreet and soothing, just suited our mood—we were too tired then for the more strenuous cosiness of British pubs. We ordered double Scotches, followed by Black Horse ale and club sandwiches. We felt marvellously relaxed. "This hotel," I said to my wife, "has restored my faith in American civilisation."

"Yes," she agreed. "You must write to the manager. The service rendered by his staff has saved all our lives this night."

"By God, I *will* write to the manager," I exclaimed happily, and ordered two more club sandwiches.

The next morning we took the Lehigh Valley Railroad's crack train, the Black Diamond, to Ithaca, and a week later, when I was settling in to the normal academic routine again, my wife reminded me about writing to the hotel manager. The impression of that enchanted service was still so vivid that I sat down there and then and wrote to the manager, describing our gruelling ordeal in disembarking, explaining our relief and joy at the friendly and considerate service rendered by the hotel, and concluded by assuring him that that service had restored a shaken faith in the American way of life. Three days later I received a reply: the manager said that in his fifteen years as manager of the hotel he had received numerous letters from guests, all complaining about one thing or another, but never before had he had a letter couched in such terms as mine; he added that most people took hotel service for granted, that it was a principle with them that the comfort and convenience of guests always had first priority and that, while he was confident that his staff did all they could to live up to this principle, he was peculiarly gratified to learn from my letter that they had met this emergency so adequately. He concluded by asking whether I would object to his reading my letter to to the staff meeting next Friday, and by sending his remembrances to Professor Meek, head of the Hotel School at Cornell.

This was satisfactory all round. I freely gave the manager permission to read my letter at his staff meeting, and in reply received a note assuring me that if at any time he (the manager) could be of service to me, I must let him know.

That was September. The following December, just after Christmas, the annual meeting of the Modern Language Association took place at the same hotel, and I duly reserved my humble five-dollar special-price-to-professors room. It never occurred to me to ask any special favours from the manager, as I had taken his offer of future courtesies as a mere friendly matter of form. I arrived at the hotel on the evening of 26 December, and took possession of my five-dollar room.

The next morning, breakfasting at the coffee shop, I ran into a colleague of mine and his wife. "Hello," I said, "I thought you weren't coming to the M.L.A. this year."

"We weren't." he replied. "We were going to spend the vacation at New Haven with my mother. But we decided at the last minute to come here. We phoned down for a reservation from Cornell yesterday afternoon."

206

"What!" I said. "With all these conventions going on here, and the hotel bulging at the seams, you were able to get a double room at a moment's notice?"

"Why yes," he said. "I asked for the manager, and told him I was a close friend of the Professor Daiches who had written him that nice letter." (I had told that story around Cornell.) "And he gave us what looks very like the bridal suite. A lovely set of rooms. You must come up and see them."

"And for the regular academic price of five dollars," put in his wife.

"Well I'm damned," I replied, for I could think of nothing else to say. I felt annoyed that someone else had cashed in on my adventure, while I was left with my very ordinary little room.

"You should take people up on their offers," went on my colleague. "Follow up your contacts. That's the secret of success in modern life."

"Bah!" I said, and went back to my room: I found it looking positively tiny.

On 29 December, having spent the previous evening dining magnificently with some old friends at the St Denis restaurant, where we had consumed vast quantities of Alsatian *vin gris*, I found that my cash was running low: I hadn't enough, in fact, to pay for my hotel room. There were several people in New York who would have cashed a cheque for me, but this time I decided to take advantage myself of my own connections with the manager. I entered the cashier's office, gave my name, and explained that I knew the manager and would like to cash a cheque for fifty dollars. The cashier disappeared for a few moments and came back wreathed in smiles. He wrote something on the back of my cheque and told me that if I took it round to the cash desk they would cash it for me. I took it, and they cashed it.

I was just the tiniest bit bothered about having enough money in the bank to cover the amount of the cheque. I had spent heavily in the days immediately preceding Christmas, but

I figured that I had exactly fifty-two dollars left in my account. But in any case, even supposing I had made a mistake of a few dollars (which was more than likely), the University made a practice of paying salary cheques into employees' banks the day before Christmas instead of adopting the normal practice of paying them in on the last day of the month. This was a sort of Christmas present to the faculty, and if the custom had been followed this year I would have nothing to worry about. Indeed, I forgot all about the matter until, back in Ithaca on 31 December, I rang up the bank just before closing time and asked if my salary cheque was in. Yes, I was told, all the salary cheques were in.

The telephone bell woke me as I was sleeping late on the morning of 2 January. It was Western Union, with a telegram. "Your cheque for fifty dollars returned from bank marked no funds please send fifty dollars in bills or money order registered mail immediately." It was signed by the hotel cashier.

My first reaction was extreme indignation. Someone had made a terrible blunder. I rang up the bank, and demanded angrily to speak to the manager. After a long argument, I was left with the information that my cheque from New York had arrived at the bank on the morning of the 31st, and my salary cheque had been paid in on the afternoon of the 31st. There were forty-nine dollars and two cents left in my account when my cheque for fifty dollars was presented. They therefore had no option but to send back the cheque. To my protest that he must have known that my salary cheque was due in any moment, and that to bounce a man's cheque in the circumstances for a mere ninety-eight cents was not gentlemanly behaviour, the manager turned a deaf ear. What he did was routine procedure, he said. I told him that this could not conceivably have happened in Britain (which was true; as a student at Oxford I was continually overdrawing inadvertently and never had a cheque stopped).

I put down the receiver and dialled Western Union. I had to reassure the hotel cashier somehow. I apparently got the same girl who had read me the upsetting telegram a few moments before.

"I want to send a telegram," I said, searching in my mind for suitable words. What I really wanted to say was that my faith in American civilisation, so beautifully restored by the hotel manager that evening in September, had been shattered again by the bank manager. But I couldn't quite say that, and I fumbled in my dictation.

"Deeply distressed," I began, "at unhappy accident resulting in my cheque being returned marked 'no funds'. Wish to assure you—"

"Listen," said the Western Union girl, interrupting me in a kindly tone. "You don't have to say all that. It'll just cost you more."

"But they bounced a cheque I cashed at the hotel," I said, in an anguished voice, "and I've got to explain."

"Listen," she said again. "Have you got enough money in the bank now?"

"Yes," I said.

"Sure?" she asked, but with no offence in her tone.

"Yes, I'm sure."

"Well then," she said, "just say: 'Cheque good. Re-deposit.' "

"But oughtn't I to explain—"

"Explain nothing," she said. " 'Cheque good. Re-deposit' will do the trick. That's what they always say."

"Is that really all I need to say?" I asked.

"Of course," she said. "Don't think you're the first one. I'll send it as 'Cheque good. Re-deposit' and put your name after it. You won't hear any more about it. 'Bye." And she hung up. My faith in America was restored once more.

I know I have got all the details of this series of episodes right, because I wrote it all up shortly afterwards as an amusing anecdote I might want some day to publish. I present it here because it symbolises very accurately the extremes of appreciation and indignation with which, all through our years in the United States, we reacted to American life. By the time we were settled in Ithaca, my wife and I knew America intimately enough to have lost all that initial combination of bewilderment, admiration, annoyance, excitement and general sense of superiority with which most visitors from Britain used to face the country. We felt that we understood its history, its society, its faults and its virtues. Although we did not want to become Americans, there were lots of things about the country for which we had developed a great affection. At the same time every now and again some well-known feature of American behaviour would provoke in one or other of us (more often in me than in my wife) a short tempest of anger, which reflected the frustration of the exile. And when we finally came home for good, we would allow no one except ourselves to abuse the Americans.

My years at Cornell were full and productive. I taught a great variety of courses, several of which eventually produced books: my seminar on eighteenth-century Scottish literature produced my Burns book; my lectures on Milton produced much later my book on Milton; and my lectures on the history of literary criticism produced my *Critical Approaches to Literature*. It was while I was at Cornell, too, that I made my first venture into American literature. Victor Reynolds, head of Cornell University Press, came into my office at the University one day (American professors have "offices" while British professors have "rooms") and asked me what I thought of Willa Cather. I replied that I had only read one novel of hers, and that was a long time ago. He then offered to lend me her complete works if I would go through them and then decide whether I would like to write a critical book about her. I had never before undertaken to write a book to order in this way, but the suggestion intrigued me, and I borrowed Willa Cather's novels and read them all through, first rapidly one after the other then a second time slowly and carefully. I found them interesting, and I saw a pattern in them which I thought I should like to trace, so I agreed to write the book, which was published by Cornell University Press in 1950. This explains why I wrote in my preface that the book was written to answer the question: "What do you think of the novels of Willa Cather?" What I did not say in the preface was that when I was first asked that question I had read almost nothing of Willa Cather's work.

For some years I was a regular reviewer of new poetry for the *New York Herald-Tribune* Sunday book section, and this kept me in touch with what was happening among the younger poets, especially the younger American poets. At the same time, as Chairman of the Division of Literature and member of some important policy-making committees at Cornell, I occupied an important place within the University. Indeed, I don't think that I have ever quite enjoyed again the reputation I had at Cornell. Being in a sense an outsider, trained in a quite different educational system, and being (I believe) the youngest full professor on the arts side, I had rather a special position. Of course there were many other Cornell professors who had come from abroad, but these had for the most part settled in America and deliberately put down roots there. I remained a bit peripheral, very British (or rather, European) in orientation and commitment, yet at the same time I don't think it is an exaggeration to say that I was a Cornell institution. Certainly, whenever I return there for a visit, as I do periodically, I discover legends about myself circulating, some of which contain only a very small germ of truth.

It was on 23 October 1950 that I learned that I had been appointed University Lecturer at Cambridge, as from the beginning of the next academic year. I knew that it would be like starting a whole new career for myself. I foresaw (and rightly, as it turned out) that at the beginning at least I would be more of an outsider at Cambridge than I had been at Cornell. It was a long time since I had any personal experience of British universities. My undergraduate years at Edinburgh were a world away, and my years as graduate student and research fellow at Oxford seemed equally distant. But, for all my affection for Cornell, I never doubted that I was right to leave when I did.

A Third World

Most of my American academic friends were deeply puzzled by my decision. I could understand the administration's attitude, which I have recorded in an earlier chapter, but it was surprising that many Anglophile Americans, who knew and loved England and her literature, thought that I was quite crazy to think of settling again in England when I had a chance of staying permanently in America and becoming an American citizen. The wife of one former Chicago colleague, a very old friend, said simply, "You're mad". But I knew that I had either to take the Cambridge position or else reconcile myself to being always a visitor whenever I went home, and this neither my wife nor I could bring ourselves to do. One could not go on indefinitely saying that one would return home permanently in the near future. Thirteen years had elapsed since that calm Sunday morning when we had first seen the American shore from the deck of the *Tuscania*.

So we turned home in the summer of 1951, to start, in a sense, all over again. Except for my books, we had sold nearly all our possessions before leaving, for the cost of transporting them proved prohibitive. We had virtually no money saved up, for we had spent everything we could save in coming home to Scotland every second summer. We owned no house and no furniture, and I had not even accumulated any pension rights since I had cashed in the proceeds of my American pension payments in order to find the money to support my family between leaving Cornell and drawing my first salary from Cambridge (who paid quarterly, so that it was not due till Christmas). We were indeed beginning again, and this time with three children. I found the prospect exciting. I have always had a periodic impulse to start afresh, and I was certainly doing that now. I had lived in two worlds as a child, found a third world in America as a young man, and was now returning in my thirty-ninth year to see if I could synthesise my experiences anew in my native country.

INDEX

Abercrobie, Lascelles, 187
Abrams, M. H., 179, 180-81
Abramson, Ben, 104
A.E. (George Russell), 188
Archibald, George, 1st Baron, 141
Auden, W. H., 59

Babbitt, Irving, 2
Bailey, Liberty Hyde, 156
Bald, R. C., 156
Balfour, Sir John, 117
Bender, Albert, 80
Bennett, J. A. W., 91, 111
Bentley, Eric, 111
Bentley, G. E., 28, 72, 78
Bentley, Phyllis, 141
Benton, William, 149-50
Berlin, Irving, 118-19
Berlin, Sir Isaiah, 111, 117-19, 121
Bishop, Morris, 182
Black, Max, 179
Blair, Walter and Carol, 66-67
Bloom, Harold, 180
Borgese, G. A., 28-30, 72
Breadloaf, Vermont, 44
Brinnin, John M., 192
British Embassy, Washington, 91, 105, 109, 113-37
British Information Services, New York, 91, 103-4, 110-12, 123, 128, 140
Brooks, Cleanth, 42, 58
Burns, Robert, 51, 103, 177
Butler, Sir Harold, 121, 128, 129, 138

Calder, Angus, 92, 98

Cambridge, 9, 39, 81 158 211-12
Caxton Club, The, 102-3
Cazamian, Louis, 55
Chappaqua, N.Y., 112-13
Chicago, 6-37, 72, 84, 111
Chicago School of Criticism, 27, 42
Chicago Tribune, 33
Chicago, University of, 7-15, 21-36, 38-46, 52, 87-88, 99, 111, 159-60
Churchill, Sir Winston, 113, 118-19, 130
Clark, William, 93
Cooper, Lane, 156
Cornell University, 153-60, 161, 175-92, 212
Cousins, Norman, 188
Cowell, Frank, 151
Crane, R. S., 11, 21-28, 41, 42, 44, 52, 55, 56-57
Crosby, Caresse, 135
Cruikshank, Robin, 140
Cullen, Banffshire, 164-74, 175

Daiches, Alan, 46, 163-64, 193-199
Daiches, Elizabeth (Mrs Derek Austin), 167-72, 193, 198
Daiches, Jennifer (Mrs Angus Calder), 165-66, 197, 198
Daiches, L. H., Q.C., 163
Davidson, Donald, 44
Day, Edmund E., 63
Dill, Field-Marshal Sir John, 127-28
Donne, John, 55
Duthie, G. I., 157

Index

Early Birds Breakfast Club, 105-9
Edinburgh, University of, 1, 11, 38, 41, 42, 49, 53, 56, 58, 211
Einaudi, Mario, 179
Eisenhower, General D., 123
Eliot, T. S., 53, 54, 59, 61, 189
Empson, William 25-26

Faust, Clarence, 26
Flint, Mrs Edith Foster, 28
Flint, F. S., 189
Ford, Edith, 121, 151
Forster, E. M., 81
Frost, Robert, 186-90

Gardner, Neville, 132
Grierson, Sir Herbert, 1, 55, 56, 157

Halevi, Judah, 45
Halifax, Edward Wood, 1st Earl of, 113, 115-17, 127
Hamilton, Hamish, 141
Harmsworth, Desmond, 110-11
Hedrick, U. P., 16
Homer, 52-53, 135
Horizon, 97
Hulme, T. E., 53, 59, 189
Huntington Library, 78-79
Hutchins, R. M., 13-14, 24, 27, 160, 179
Huxley, Aldous, 55

Joyce, James, 45, 55, 61, 64, 105

Keats, John, 52
Kelly, Mayor, 37
Keyes, Admiral of the Fleet Lord, 123-26
Keynes, J. M., 130-31
Kitchin, George, 39

La Follette, Robert, 34
Lawrence, D. H., 61
Leavis, F. R., 1, 39, 41, 61
Left Book Club, 32, 97
Lehmann, John, 98
Literature and Society, 32
Lovett, R. M., 35
Lowell, Amy, 187-88

McCormick, R. R., 33
MacDiarmid, Hugh, 51
McGill University, 157-58
McKeon, Richard, 11, 22, 27, 40, 41, 42
Maclean, Donald, 119-20
MacLeish, Archibald, 149
MacNeice, Louis, 98-99
Mair, A. W., 14
Marvel, Tom, 16
Maugham, Somerset, 104, 113
Memphis, Tennessee, 68-70
Middleton, Sir George, 119
Miller, Henry, 104
Minden, Nevada, 76
Moore, Harry T., 135

Nabokov, Vladimir, 182-86
New Literary Values, 41
New Orleans, 72
New Republic, The, 94
New York City, 3, 4, 5-6, 7, 36
New Yorker, The, 64
Newton, David, 133
Nicholas, Herbert, 141
Nicoll, Allardyce, 132
Novel and the Modern World, The, 23, 46, 64, 94, 153

O'Neill, Eugene, 2
Osborn, J. M., 92, 94-95
Oxford, 2, 4, 8, 11, 12, 13, 14, 32, 33, 38, 39, 42, 49, 50, 51, 53, 54, 56, 59, 211

Index

Pasadena, California, 78-79
Penguin New Writing, 97, 98
Place of Meaning in Poetry, The, 53, 56
Poetry, 59, 64, 98, 153
Poetry and the Modern World, 64-65
Port Clyde, Maine, 95
Pound, Ezra, 55, 187-88

Raines, Claud, 146
Raphael, Chaim 111
Raphael, D. D., 133-34
Riesman, David, 93
Robinson, F. N., 2
Roosevelt, President F. D., 1, 2, 33, 36, 129-30, 136-37
Runyon, Damon, 128-29

San Francisco, 72, 79-80
Schaffner, Mrs Sarah, 28-32, 80
Schoonmaker, Frank, 16, 17
Scott, Sir Walter, 51
Sebeok, Thomas 36
Shelley, P. B., 52
Stevenson, R. L., 24, 48, 49, 50, 51
Strachey, John, 32, 97

Tate, Allen, 94
Thomas, Dylan, 190-92
Thomas, Edward, 187
Thompson, Denys, 1
Thompson, H. W., 156
Twain, Mark, 7
Twitty, Tom, 131-32

UNESCO, 148-50

Vigney, Alfred de, 52

Wagner, Philip, 16
Whitman, Walt, 48, 73
Wilder, Thornton, 135
Willcox, W. F., 156
Williamson, George, 46
Wilson, Dover, 132, 140
Wilson, Stanley, 102
Wilt, Napier, 66-72
Wines, American, 16-19
Women's clubs, 47
Woolf, Virginia, 55
Wright, Sir Michael, 115, 148-149, 175

Yeats, W. B., 58, 61 187